# A CHARTER
# OF
# WORKERS' RIGHTS

# A CHARTER
# OF
# WORKERS' RIGHTS

**EDITED BY K D EWING
AND
JOHN HENDY QC**

**THE INSTITUTE OF EMPLOYMENT RIGHTS
LONDON**

This publication, like all publications of the Institute,
represents not the collective views of the Institute but only the views
of the authors. The responsibility of the Institute is limited to
approving its publication as worthy of consideration within the
labour movement.

Institute of Employment Rights
177 Abbeville Road, London SW4 9RL
020 7498 6919, fax 020 7498 9080
ier@gn.apc.org, www.ier.org.uk

First published 2002

Copyright © Institute of Employment Rights
2002

The authors have asserted their rights under the Copyright, Designs
and Patents Act, 1988, to be identified as authors of this work.

ISBN 1 873271 97 2

British Library Cataloguing in Publication data
A catalogue record for this book is available from the British Library

Designed and typeset by the Institute of Employment Rights
Printed by Gemini Press Limited, West Sussex

# Contents

# The contributors

**Keith Ewing** is President of the Institute of Employment Rights. He is Professor of Public Law at King's College London.

**John Hendy QC** is a barrister at Old Square Chambers specialising in labour law; Chairman of the Institute of Employment Rights; Visiting Professor at King's College London; Vice-Chairman of the Employment Law Bar Association; a Vice-President of the International Centre for Trade Union Rights and a Senior Commissioner of the International Labour Rights Commission.

**Jon Cruddas MP** is Labour member for Dagenham.

**Simon Deakin** is Robert Monks Professor of Corporate Governance at the University of Cambridge and an Executive Committee member of the Institute of Employment Rights.

**Jeremy Dear** is General Secretary of the National Union of Journalists.

**Jill Earnshaw** is Senior Lecturer in Employment Law at Manchester School of Management, UMIST.

**Gary Fabian** is Team Organiser (Policy Unit) at train drivers' union ASLEF.

**Michael Ford** is a barrister at Old Square Chambers and an Executive Committee member of the Institute of Employment Rights.

**Andy Freer** is a solicitor at Pattinson & Brewer Solicitors.

**Gregor Gall** is a Reader in Industrial Relations at the University of Stirling.

**Steve Gibbons** is editor of the *Legal Brief* at Incomes Data Services.

**Sarah Hannett** is a Lecturer in Law at King's College London, and an Executive Committee member of Lesbian and Gay Employment Rights (LAGER).

**Philip James** is Professor of Employment Relations at Middlesex University and a member of the Executive Committee of the Institute of Employment Rights.

**Carolyn Jones** is Director of the Institute of Employment Rights.

**Professor Sue Konzelmann** is Senior Research Fellow in the ESRC Centre for Business Research at Cambridge University and Associate Professor in the School of Business and Economics at Indiana University South Bend.

**Mike Lawson** is National Officer (Political) at the fire service union FBU.

**David Lewis** is Professor of Employment Law at Middlesex University.

**Aileen McColgan** is Professor of Human Rights Law at King's College London, a member of Matrix Chambers and an Executive Committee member of the Institute.

**Professor Jonathan Michie** is the Sainsbury Chair of Management at Birkbeck, University of London and an Executive Committee member of the Institute of Employment Rights.

**Karon Monaghan** is a barrister at Matrix Chambers and an Executive Committee member of the Institute of Employment Rights.

**Richard Nobles** is a Reader in Law at the London School of Economics.

**Peter Nolan** is the Montague Burton Professor of Industrial Relations at Leeds University Business School.

**Dr Tonia Novitz** is a Lecturer in Law at the University of Bristol and was a Marie Curie Fellow at the European University Institute 2001-2.

**Joe O'Hara** is National Legal Officer of GMB and an Executive Committee member of the Institute of Employment Rights.

**John O'Regan** is the Political Advisor to the Graphical Paper and Media Union.

**Bob Simpson** is Reader in Law at the London School of Economics and a member of the Institute of Employment Rights.

**Gary Slater**

**Dave Tarren** is Research Officer at the Graphical Paper and Media Union.

**Roger Walden** is a lecturer in Employment Law in Manchester School of Management at UMIST.

**Ivan Walker** is a partner in Thompsons Solicitors, and is head of their Pensions Department.

**Roger Welch** is a Principal Lecturer in Employment Law at the University of Portsmouth, a member of NATFHE and has written extensively on trade union issues.

**Frank Wilkinson** is a visiting professor at Birkbeck College and an Executive Committee member of the Institute of Employment Rights.

**Professor Geoff Wood** is Professor of Comparative Human Resource Management at Middlesex University.

**Sarah Veale** is Senior Employment Rights Officer at the TUC.

# Foreword

John Monks, TUC General Secretary

A T the 2001 TUC Congress, a resolution on employment rights was carried overwhelmingly. It acknowledged the progress which had been made since the election of a Labour government in 1997 but pointed to a number of areas where reforms were still needed to achieve "Fairness at Work" for all workers. In particular, the resolution noted that the government still had some way to go to ensure that UK workers enjoyed the same standard of protection as workers in most other EU member states.

The government is now engaged on a series of consultation exercises on issues of central importance, including the transposition of the EU Directive on Information and Consultation, the review of the Employment Relations Act 1999 and the review of employment status. It is important that the trade union movement engages fully in these consultation exercises and lobbies for the improvements set out in the 2001 Congress resolution. To this end, I warmly welcome this new publication from the IER, in which a number of highly respected experts look at the issues which are identified in the TUC policy. The Charter also clearly locates the issues within the current economic context and tackles the arguments about labour market regulation and productivity. I hope that this Charter will be widely read and discussed in the trade union movement in coming months as we continue our campaign for Fairness at Work.

# Chapter 1

# The foundations of a workers' charter

1.1 TUC Congress in 2001 resolved to establish and promote a Charter of Workers' Rights. The Institute of Employment Rights, though not a campaigning body, has drawn together a group of experts amongst academics, practising lawyers and trade union officials to publish ideas for a new workers' charter for consideration by the trade union movement and the TUC. Only the labour movement can decide upon the contents of such a Charter. But a charter of workers' rights should not be controversial – at least amongst workers, trade unionists and those who have studied international labour law: it should be founded on fundamental values. They are not plucked out of the air, rather they are derived from well established and numerous international law documents which have been ratified by the UK.

## International standards

1.2 The international instruments (as lawyers refer to them) which contain labour laws (and the social values and purposes which underpin them) include the following: the *United Nations Charter* and the *UN Declaration of Human Rights* 1948; the *International Covenant on Economic, Social and Cultural Rights* 1966; the *Council of Europe's Social Charter* of 1961 (revised 1996); the *European Community Charter of the Fundamental Social Rights of Workers* of 1989; and the *Charter of Fundamental Rights of the European Union* of 2000. They are found in the *Conventions* and *Recommendations* of the *International Labour Organisation* and its *Declaration of Fundamental Principles and Rights at Work* of 1998; and in the OECD *Guidelines for*

*Multinational Enterprises* of 2000. It will be seen that though some of these sources are long standing others are very modern indeed, as is the UK's endorsement of them.

The **Constitution of the International Labour Organisation,** established in 1919 begins with three fundamentals:
— *universal and lasting peace can be established only if it is based upon social justice;*
— *conditions of labour exist involving such injustice, hardship and privation to large numbers of people as to produce unrest so great that the peace and harmony of the world are imperilled; and an improvement of those conditions is urgently required; as, for example, by the regulation of the hours of work, including the establishment of a maximum working day and week, the regulation of the labour supply, the prevention of unemployment, the provision of an adequate living wage, the protection of the worker against sickness, disease and injury arising out of his employment, the protection of children, young persons and women, provision for old age and injury, …recognition of the principle of freedom of association, …and other measures;*
— *the failure of any nation to adopt humane conditions of labour is an obstacle in the way of other nations which desire to improve the conditions in their own countries.*

The ILO **Declaration of Philadelphia** 1944 reaffirmed the fundamental principles of the ILO and, in particular, that:
— *labour is not a commodity;*
— *freedom of expression and of association are essential to sustained progress;*
— *poverty anywhere constitutes a danger to prosperity everywhere;*
and committed the ILO to the goals of: full employment and the raising of standards of living; satisfying work; training; wages and earnings, hours and other conditions of work calculated to ensure a just share of the fruits of progress to all, and a minimum living wage to all in need of such protection; the effective recognition of the right of collective bargaining, and other matters.

The ILO's **Declaration on Fundamental Principles and Rights at Work** 1998 included the fundamental propositions that:
— *economic growth is essential but not sufficient to ensure equity, social progress and the eradication of poverty, confirming the need for the ILO to promote strong social policies, justice and democratic institutions;*
— *in seeking to maintain the link between social progress and economic growth, the guarantee of fundamental principles and rights at work is of particular significance in that it enables the persons concerned to claim freely and on the basis of equality of opportunity their fair share of the wealth which they have helped to generate, and to achieve fully their human potential;*

> The **United Nations Charter** proclaims that:
> *we the peoples of the United Nations determined to... reaffirm faith in fundamental human rights, in the dignity and worth of the human person, in the equal rights of men and women... and to establish conditions under which justice and respect for the obligations arising from treaties and other sources of international law can be maintained, and to promote social progress and better standards of life in larger freedom, and for these ends to ...employ international machinery for the promotion of the economic and social advancement of all peoples.*
>
> It demands *"universal respect for, and observance of, human rights and fundamental freedoms for all without distinction as to race, sex, language, or religion."*
>
> The United Nations **Declaration of Human Rights** 1948 states as its first premise that *"recognition of the inherent dignity and of the equal and inalienable rights of all members of the human family is the foundation of freedom, justice and peace in the world."*

> The **International Covenant on Economic, Social and Cultural Rights** 1966 states at the outset that *"the ideal of free human beings enjoying freedom from fear and want can only be achieved if conditions are created whereby everyone may enjoy his economic, social and cultural rights, as well as his civil and political rights."*

1.3 So the values to shape a modern workers' charter can be seen to be derived from universal and absolute standards adopted across the civilised world. And these standards have immediate application to workplace realities. It is true that international laws ratified by the British government do not automatically become part of UK national law – and there is no international police force to make governments abide by the international labour laws they have signed up to. But in a new development, the ILO and European Social Charter decisions on ratified labour law will become part of British law because they are now relied upon by the European Court of Human Rights which administers the European Convention of Human Rights and Fundamental Freedoms which was itself expressly incorporated into UK law by the Human Rights Act 1998.

> The **European Court of Human Rights** held in the *Wilson and Palmer* case (discussed in chapter 7 below):
> *Under United Kingdom law at the relevant time it was, therefore, possible for an employer effectively to undermine or frustrate a trade union's ability to strive for the protection of its members' interests. The Court notes that this aspect of domestic law has been the subject of criticism by Social Charter's Committee*

*of Independent Experts and the ILO's Committee on Freedom of Association. It considers that, by permitting employers to use financial incentives to induce employees to surrender important union rights, the respondent State failed in its positive obligation to secure the enjoyment of the rights under Article 11 of the Convention. This failure amounted to a violation of Article 11, as regards both the applicant unions and the individual applicants.*

# A modern charter for a modern workplace

1.4 A modern, efficient employment relationship founded on international standards will involve a change in the balance of power between employer and worker. It will displace the Victorian notions of "master and servant" – where the master is in complete dominance over the subordinated servant – which continues to influence government and employer thinking. Such an employment relationship is not just antiquely grotesque, it is also foolishly uneconomic, as chapters 2 and 3 show. In order to overcome these old fashioned values and to rectify the imbalance of power, laws which have done so much to embed management prerogative, dis-empower workers and restrict unions' ability to represent their members effectively must be repealed. In their place must be laws which guarantee the fundamental rights of trade unions and trade unionists, laws which give workers the essential protections and entitlements which are necessary in a modern society.

1.5 The contemporary nature of a charter is important. A modern charter must be appropriate to deal with modern problems, such as the issue of globalisation – a problem identified in the core documents above but now felt much more acutely as the multi-nationals use modern technology and economic power to play off one part of the globe against another. A charter must be modern enough to deal with the current need to defend public services against privatisation with its consequent degeneration of terms of employment, loss of employment, degradation of public services, and the imposition on taxpayers and consumers of the burden of funding the profiteers. On the other hand a charter should not be addressed to transient needs. Its fundamental principles must be true and relevant whatever the state of the economic cycle or the political complexion of the government.

## Modern values for a modern charter

1.6 A modern charter drawn from the principles of international law must be based on modern values. To this end a number of core values of contemporary significance can be clearly identified:

## Social inclusion by social justice

A key function of a modern charter is to ensure that workers are adequately and fairly rewarded for the work they are employed to do, and the wealth they help to create. Income from work ought also to be a principal way of reducing inequalities in society, which in turn is essential to a democratic culture and the integration of all citizens into the social fabric and political life of the nation.

## Equality of opportunity

One of the main aims of a workers' charter is to ensure that everyone who enters the labour market has an opportunity to fulfil their full potential. Workers should not be excluded from employment on irrational or arbitrary grounds unrelated to their abilities. But it also means that barriers to effective labour market participation should be fully addressed, and that workers have meaningful access to training and learning opportunities.

## Dignity and respect

Dignity as a principle is slippery and elusive. But as its core it means that workers should be protected from treatment by employers, fellow workers, or other third parties which damages what one commentator has referred to as their "self respect and physical or moral integrity". This would prohibit any form of bullying and harassment of workers, as well as any unreasonable surveillance which has not been authorised by the worker.

## Participation and democracy

In a democratic society people ought to be permitted to participate in all rule-making processes by which they are governed, and to be involved in any decision which will have significant implications for themselves and their families. Collective bargaining is the most effective method of participation at the workplace, since it ensures an independent voice for workers through representative institutions.

## Freedom and solidarity

Here the principal concern is the need to ensure the freedom of workers to act together for mutual support through trade unions without State or employer interference. This is fundamental for any workers' charter, with trade unions being the prime means by which the imbalance of power between worker and employer can be addressed. To this end it is important that workers should be free to support others in need.

## Fairness and security

A final concern relates to the need for workers to be treated fairly. This applies across the employment relationship: from hiring, to the determination of employment conditions, to the application of discretion by employers (such as overtime and promotion), to the handling of grievances, to the taking of disciplinary action, to the termination of the employment relationship.

1.7 These core values inform much of the analysis and recommenations that follow. But it is important to note that they are not mutually exclusive but mutually dependent and overlapping. For example, social justice requires people to be treated with dignity and respect, and it would be difficult to contend that the dignity of the worker was being respected by a regime which denied him or her a voice in the decisions by which he or she would be affected while at work. The overlapping and interdependent nature of these values was fully recognised by the Director General of the ILO in 2001 when he said:

"The goal of decent work is best expressed through the eyes of people. It is about your job and future prospects; about your working conditions; about balancing work and family life, putting your kids through school or getting them out of child labour. It is about gender equality, equal recognition, and enabling women to make choices and take control of their lives. It is about your personal abilities to compete in the market place, keep up with new technological skills and remain healthy. It is about developing your entrepreneurial skills, about receiving a fair share of the wealth that you have helped to create and not being discriminated against; it is about having a voice in your workplace and your community. In the most extreme situations it is about moving from subsistence to existence. For many, it is the primary route out of poverty. For many more it is about realising personal ambitions in their daily existence and about solidarity with others. And everywhere, and for everybody, decent work is about securing human dignity."[1]

---

1  *Reducing the Decent Work Deficit: A Global Challenge,* ILO Director General's Report, 2001

# An enforceable Charter

1.8 A charter of workers' rights will be worthless if it is simply regarded as a ringing declaration. It must identify the legal and other tools (including industrial action) to ensure that the charter rights are effective and can be enforced. Legal procedures to do so are needed. And of course the acquisition by unions of the human rights which international law requires them to be given will improve their power in workplaces to ensure that workers' rights are enforced there without resort to the law. One of the main problems with the international standards referred to above and throughout this book is that many of them, though ratified by the UK, are not enforceable and are merely paid lip service by successive governments. It is therefore essential that the international laws which the UK has ratified (and it has a good record on ratification) must be implemented in our national laws. This will ensure that workers can enjoy their protection and enforce them against employers who seek to gain competitive advantage by adopting lower standards than in other countries. Indeed, by the adoption in the UK of a workers' charter compliant with international law, this country would set an example which might lead to the implementation of these civilised minimum standards to the millions of workers throughout the world exploited by globalisation. This could be achieved by making international trade and international trade agreements conditional on international labour standards. But a first step for the UK must be the implementation of these standards in this country.

# Chapter 2

# The economic case for a workers' charter

2.1 Workers' rights are crucial for both economic efficiency and social justice. Properly constituted, workers' rights create a balance of power in the workplace, in organisations and in the wider society. This in turn improves the creation, development, and use of productive resources, and prevents their dissipation in unemployment and poverty. For these reasons it is necessary to have laws which legitimise and promote the role of trade unions and collective bargaining on the one hand, and establish legally binding minimum terms and conditions of employment on the other.[1] These rights address the imbalance of power between labour and capital to be found in unrestricted markets, which otherwise guarantee workers little more than the freedom to be exploited.

## The failure of liberal economics

2.2 The need for laws and institutions guaranteeing workers rights is denied by neo-liberals who claim that unconstrained markets deliver economic justice. Neo-liberalism is a restatement of the core beliefs of liberal economics, which evolved to justify capitalist freedom. It is a utopian vision of self-regulating markets which transform the inherent selfishness of individuals into general good. The market provides the opportunity and incentives for individuals to exploit to the full their property (labour in the case of workers) but prevents them from exploiting any advantage they might have by

1 For these reasons it is also necessary to promote full employment as a primary policy objective, as well as the provision of health care, education and social support.

throwing them into competition with others. For neo-liberals, market forces by these means deliver distributional justice and optimal economic welfare and this gives them supremacy over man-made laws and institutions. Unless these conform to the laws of the market they risk being in *restraint of trade* and economically damaging. From the neo-liberal perspective a workers' charter is unnecessary; workers' rights are guaranteed by the market.

2.3 The extension of trade union and workers rights was increasingly questioned by neo-liberals as inflation accelerated in the post-war period. They gave renewed emphasis to traditional liberal arguments that such interventions were against the laws of the market and caused serious economic damage, leading to a *neo-liberal* revival. In the UK, the Tory government adopted a neo-liberal economic strategy in 1979. Since then, macro-economic policy has been dominated by monetary control targeted at inflation, whilst responsibility for industrial performance has been increasingly delegated to the market. Full employment has been abandoned as a policy objective, trade unions have been weakened, legal control of minimum labour standards relaxed, and out-of-work benefits reduced to increase labour market *flexibility* to allow employers to adjust wage costs to their immediate needs. Concurrently, product markets and business have been deregulated and taxes on the rich have been cut to encourage enterprise.

2.4 It was claimed that the removal of workers' rights and the strengthening of the hands of their employers would improve economic performance and that the prosperity would *trickle-down* the income distribution so as to compensate those below for sacrifices they had been called upon to make. But these expectations have not been fulfilled. Poverty dramatically increased in the 18 years of Tory rule. Unemployment increased more than threefold despite substantial reductions in the relative pay of the lowest paid, increased job insecurity, cuts in unemployment benefits, and added pressure on the unemployed to take jobs on any terms. The consequent impoverishment of a growing proportion of the population increased the social welfare bill so that government expenditure constantly threatened to spiral out of control despite the cuts in individual entitlement, pruning of the welfare state and wholesale selling off of public assets. As a result, the increasingly under-resourced public sector has staggered under the growing demands made upon it.

2.5 New Labour embraced neo-liberalism, and when it came to power in 1997 adopted and developed the Tory neo-liberal agenda. Parsimonious Tory spending plans were retained together with their pro-business stance, and New Labour went further than the Tories in delegating responsibility for interest rate determination to the Bank of England and in imposing a requirement to work on to entitlement to welfare benefits. Less in the neo-liberal mould, a minimum wage was introduced to put into effect a long established Labour Party commitment, but it was set at such a low level to meet business demands that it did little more than legitimise low pay. Similarly, concessions on employment regulation and worker representation have been kept small in the interest of maintaining labour market flexibility, a euphemism for low wages and poor working conditions. The weakening of workers' rights has been a crucial element in the policy reforms of the past three decades. The failure of these policies to deliver what was promised invites a reconsideration of the role of workers' rights, the effect of their removal, and whether they should be reintroduced, extended and redesigned.

## Liberal economics and the employment relationship

2.6 The 1979 Conservative government's response to competitive failure was to remove restrictions on managers' right to manage by eroding trade union, worker and social welfare rights. The failure of this *macho* approach to stem the continued decline in UK competitiveness explains why, especially after 1990, more and more companies turned to increasingly co-operative forms of work organisation. Following this trend, New Labour endorsed labour-management 'partnership' as an effective approach for improving industrial performance. However, because no serious attempt has been made to remedy the power imbalance that facilitates managerial prerogative, New Labour policies (rather than rhetoric) remain wedded to a confrontational business model. This is justified by the *boss knows best* doctrines of labour management and neo-liberal dogmas of the superiority of unrestricted market forces.

2.7 Central to the debate about 'partnership' are questions regarding the extent of the mutuality of employer and employee interests, and how employee interests in partnerships should be represented. The neo-liberal tradition is that control must rest squarely in the hands of management, although ideas about how that control should be used have changed as the theory and practice of labour management have evolved. The need to exercise power over labour in order to maximise productivity and profitability has been a driving force in the development of theory and practice in labour management. From the belief that *arbitrary* managerial control was necessary to discipline recalcitrant workers, through the application of engineering principles in the *scientific management* of work, to the use of socio-psychological methods to secure worker compliance by the *human relations school*, managerial power finds support.

2.8 Liberal economics justifies the need for close supervision and stern discipline in its assumption that workers are inherently untrustworthy so that markets need supporting by managerial command. Frederick Taylor was also pre-occupied by the supposed problem of worker unreliability and found the answer in complete managerial control over the tasks of individual workers and how they should be organised and performed.[2] This is made possible, he argued, by the application of engineering laws governing production, which the *scientific management school* claimed to have discovered and developed. In their turn, the *human relations school* provided their support for managerial prerogative by applying sociological and psychological theory to labour control and motivation. Importantly then, both the scientific management and human relations schools claim to have uncovered scientific bases for understanding organisations as unitary systems in which mutuality of interests prevail, in which common interests are mediated by management, and which dispose of the need for trade unions and collective bargaining. This is echoed in *human resource management* (HRM) where the role of collective bargaining (if any) is seen as 'integrative' rather than 'distributive'. Rather than opposing management, trade unions are expected to assume the role of co-ordinators of the strategic process. The aim is to facilitate the achievement of managerial objectives, which are seen as forwarding the mutual interest of all the firm's stakeholders. From this perspective, the power to manage is a vehicle for efficiency and equity, and managers serve the interests of all stakeholders.

2.9 Tony Blair, neatly summed up this position when he outlined the Labour government's primary industrial relations objectives. They require, he argued, 'nothing less than to change the culture of relations in and at work'. He stressed the need for the new culture to be: 'one of voluntary understanding and co-operation because it has been recognised that the prosperity of each (employer and employee) is bound up in the prosperity of all'. When addressing a conference to launch the TUC commitment to partnership, the Prime Minister added that 'partnership works best when it is about real goals – part of a strategy for instance for doubling business. Or bringing employee relations in line with market re-positioning. Or ending the often-meaningless ritual of annual wage squabbling.' In this conceptualisation, no reference is made to the ritual of continu-

2  See R F Hoxie, *Scientific Management and Labor* (1915).

ous squabbling over the distribution of dividends between managers or shareholders, or to the government's constant insistence on better terms for consumers. Rather, what Mr Blair clearly has in mind is the need for workers to bow to the requirements of business by meeting its production, marketing and profitability objectives. In this, he endorses the overriding importance of managerial prerogative in the Anglo/American model of capitalism.

## The myopia of liberal economics

2.10 This cosy view of managerialism in the neo-liberal vision begs the important question of whether the claim of a complete mutuality of interest is valid from the workers' point of view. There can be little disagreement regarding the benefits to be derived from close co-operation in production. Not only does it allow for the close working together needed to raise and maintain productivity, but it also fuels learning within organisations by which new information is generated, new knowledge is created and diffused, and product, process and organisational innovations are encouraged. The resulting operational and dynamic efficiencies are crucial determinants of competitive success, as are the ability to create new opportunities and respond quickly and flexibly to changing circumstances. In turn, these fuel the prosperity which forms the basis for long-term income and employment security. Close co-operation between workers and management is therefore a potent force for improving industrial performance.

2.11 It does not follow from this, however, that all the interests of managers and workers are mutual. No doubt managers and workers have common interests in the present and future prosperity of their organisation because it determines both parties' income and job security. But this mutuality cannot extend to the distribution of the income generated by the organisation because what one gets the other cannot have. Further, as value added is a joint product of the activity of all those involved in production, there is no objective method by which the contribution of any individual can be identified and suitably rewarded. In these circumstances, it is unlikely that workers will freely accept the argument that the terms and conditions of their employment should be unilaterally determined by the market or by management, especially after it has been established that responsibility for production is shared. It is completely understandable that the standard of living of workers and their families is a primary consideration in workers' decisions regarding acceptance of the terms and conditions of employment by which they were engaged.

2.12 These interests of workers and their families are clearly different from those of their employers. However, they may not be completely separate to the extent that the demands workers make are tempered by their expectations about the prospects of the organisation that employs them. At the same time, employers should have an interest in meeting the material needs of employees in order to secure their full co-operation. However, this may be qualified by their own and others' income demands. In terms of distribution then, both sides have separate interests; and managers cannot represent both. But both sides share a concern to secure an agreement, which by recognising the legitimacy of the other side's interests helps to secure their joint future. The ability to establish institutions to achieve these objectives, and in so doing release the full potential of collective enterprise, can therefore be considered to be a productive factor. *The basis for real partnership is consequently not so much asserting that there are no differences of interests, but rather, in creating ways for finding acceptable solutions to differences.*

2.13 The ability of managers to commit themselves in this way depends on the extent to which they are required to prioritise the interests of other parties than their workforce.

- In the private sector, managers are inevitably under the shadow of the shareholders' expectations and the bankers' demands.
- In the privatised utilities, managers must give priority to the demands of state regulators purportedly operating in the interests of customers.
- In the public sector, precedence has to be given to the demands of the government, which is the ultimate controller of and paymaster for the public provision.

The ability of management fully to commit themselves to long-term partnership arrangements may be similarly constrained by uncertainty about the actions of dominant suppliers and customers. The market power of large retailers, for example, and the pressure they can exert may constrain the ability of their suppliers to deal fairly with those they employ. The priorities managers are required to give to these different interests are enshrined in corporate governance, regulatory, employment and competition law. As currently constituted, the laws affecting the corporation and its practice assign low priority to the interests of workers upon which competitive performance largely depends. Regardless of their views on the matter, managers are required to put the interests of their *dominant* stakeholders first; and although requiring unconditional commitment from their employees, the commitments managers offer in exchange are often at best conditional. Consequently, workers find it difficult to trust managers, not necessarily because the latter lack integrity, but because they are obliged to give priority to the interests of others.

## The contradictions of liberal economics

2.14 Lying at the heart of this problem is a clash between the logic of production and service delivery on the one hand, and the logic of market competition on the other. In the public sector, a similar clash exists between the logic of service delivery and the logic of exchequer control. Developments in the theory of management have led to recognition of the central role of co-operation in production, and in this the importance of worker involvement and decentralisation of control over production to the shop floor. In stark contrast, the ideology of the market rests on a belief in the immutable laws of competition which when left to their own devices optimise economic welfare. This includes the concentration of industry by large and often monopolistic firms, which is justified on the grounds that, as the products of successful competition from efficient and innovating entrepreneurs, they are the consequences of the effective working of market forces. The neo-liberal position is that although the market concentrates economic power, it also yields important benefits for society in the form of technical progress and economic growth. What is good for business is also good for society, and although the excesses of dominant firms need checking, it would check economic progress if their market opportunities were unduly restricted.

2.15 These ideas lie behind the New Labour government's pro-business stance. Accordingly, it has failed to challenge the power of big business or to give greater priority to non-shareholder interests in corporate governance and stock market operations. Privatisation and private sector involvement in the public sector has also remained a central plank on the grounds of the greater efficiency of private business, despite so much evidence to the contrary. Concurrently, little has been done to improve the bargaining power of workers weakened by Tory legislation. Therefore, power has been increasingly concentrated in the hands of top management in both the public and private sectors. Their main concern is keeping the dominant stakeholder happy by downsizing and other short-term measures to cut costs and increase profits. For this purpose, skills in financial manipulation are more important than production management skills, a priority given additional weight in the private sector by stock options and performance related bonuses linked to stock market performance. This managerial ethos extends into the public sector as the government adopts private sector measures of success and imports managers from the private sector to meet these objectives.

2.16 At the same time, and in line with best HRM practice, managerial de-layering and work reorganisation have increasingly decentralised responsibility to the shopfloor. As we have seen, in this process, largely *unconditional* demands are being made of workers whilst employers' commitment to job security, and to honouring other promises made to their employees, are increasingly *conditional* on satisfying the demands of the different dominant stakeholders we have identified: shareholders, regulators and customers. Unconditional demands made by management require workers to be totally committed to organisational objectives and to collectivise their effort, while conditional promises mean that risk is individualised and that workers are readily disposable. *What this demonstrates is the fundamental contradictions between the logic of neo-liberal capitalism, where markets and managerial power are largely unrestricted; and the logic of industrial efficiency, which requires co-operative, high performance work systems.*

2.17 So far as the logic of neo-liberal capitalism is concerned, labour is regarded as a *factor of production* and wages as a *cost of production;* and both workers and wages are required to be flexible with respect to conditions in the market for labour, products and services, and stocks and shares. Consequently, the employment contract can only provide the minimum degree of protection and the scope of trade union organisation and collective bargaining needs to be restricted. By contrast, the logic of production requires workers to be full partners in production, ready to accept high levels of responsibility for operating, co-ordinating and developing production to high levels of quality and efficiency, and to be completely open with any knowledge and suggestions they might have to improve production. To be successful, this requires partnership agreements to be made real by the willingness of both sides to exercise good faith in their implementation and in their renegotiation as circumstances change. The logic of production requires that both workers and managers honour their side of the partnership agreement, but the logic of the market requires managers to readily renege on theirs.

## The role of trade unions

2.18 Perhaps the greatest damage done by free market and managerial prerogative theories is in the creation of the myth that the invisible hand of the market supported by the visible hands of managers harmonises all interests. The denial of differences of interest, and the related denial of any role for trade unions in the independent representation of worker interests, effectively rules out the development of institutions capable of resolving conflicts in acceptable ways. This means that no effective institutional framework can exist to secure closer partnership in production. As independent representatives of workers' interests, trade unions have a crucial role to play in negotiating and implementing the formal agreement and in maintaining and making industrial partnership work. It is therefore not surprising that in those firms where the *high-road* to competitive success has been most successfully adopted, there is usually a strong trade union presence. But to be effective, trade unions need to maintain the confidence of both managers and their members.

2.19 If trade unions are to maintain the confidence of management they must act as stewards of the commitment to co-operate made by the workforce. But to achieve this, they must act decisively in their members' interests, not only in formulating the original agreements but also in implementing and enforcing them. It is in this way that trade unions maintain the confidence of their members and by doing so support their commitment to partnership and their willingness to co-operate with management. This reality extends the legitimate role of unions in representing the interests of workers to the formulation of policies governing labour markets, corporate governance, stock markets and other areas that have the potential to put workers' future at risk. It is only if this future is made secure that workers can be expected fully to commit themselves to the effective cooperation in management and operations of industrial partnership that are now generally accepted as essential for competitive success. In order to achieve the role postulated, workers and their trade unions must have a sufficient platform of rights.

# Conclusion

2.20 From an economic perspective, a charter of workers' rights has two primary objectives: one productive and one protective. The productive role lies in creating the conditions in which the capabilities of working people are fully developed and used to secure the highest possible level of economic and social well-being. The protective role lies in preventing the abuse of power both by private interests and the state which by concentrating the costs of change on workers, and especially the most vulnerable amongst them, destroys the basis for realising the full productive potential of workers and work organisation. Of course, these two roles are inextricably linked. The two roles require of the workers' charter:

- The development of forms of participatory work organisation based on the close involvement of workers at all levels in the organisation and management of production;
- The re-establishing of the rights of collective bargaining over the terms and conditions of employment and the organisation of work;
- A new settlement of workers' and trade union rights to rectify the imbalance in power in markets and in the organisation of work.

A workers' charter is of course not to be seen in isolation from other economic strategies which are necessary for productive efficiency and social inclusion. But it has a crucial role to play. These other strategies are dealt with more fully in an accompanying publication.

# Chapter 3

# The *real* economy not the *new* economy

3.1 The world of work, if you believe the pundits, is in flux. The employment patterns, work processes and systems of labour regulation that shaped the experience of paid employment in the 20th century are said to be fast receding. At the extremes, some visionaries cite the end of the career and 'job for life', even the collapse of work itself. Others hold out the prospect of a new era of creative, rewarding and liberating work. The optimists claim that we are witnessing the construction of new networks of independent producers, entrepreneurs, designers and technicians that will eventually eclipse the old style command and control management systems that shaped millions of working lives in the 20th century.

3.2 This chapter evaluates the contention that the future of work resides in the 'new' and not the 'old' industrial economy that dominated the rhythms, places and patterns of work in the past. It examines in the first two of four sections the political backdrop and policy significance of the new conceptions of work and then offers a preliminary critique. The third section looks in more detail at the changing character of labour markets and occupational shifts and continuities in contemporary Britain. Section four examines Britain's past and present role in the international division of labour, and the conclusion restates the importance of grounding policy debate in an understanding of developments in the real economy. A competitive economy must break the link with low wages, poor skills and unco-operative work relations. This points unequivocally in the direction of labour market regulation of which a workers' charter forms a crucial part.

# The political context

3.3 This debate is critically important for the government as the concept of the 'New Economy' analysed here informed much of its policy agenda during Labour's first term in office. In a little reported interview on the morning the government launched its new strategy for manufacturing industry, the Trade Secretary Patricia Hewitt admitted that in Labour's first term the government placed too much emphasis on the so called 'New Economy' at the expense of Britain's manufacturing base. She stated: "We never set out to downgrade manufacturing, but in part because of all the dotcom hype, we gave the impression that manufacturing was not a priority". She criticised as mistaken the great texts of the 'New Economy' which informed the DTI's earlier Strategy Papers on the 'Knowledge Based Economy'. The political and economic significance of this shift cannot be overstated. The conception of the 'New Economy' developed during Labour's first term formed the rationale for its policy stance of limited labour market regulation.

3.4 This change of policy invites reconsideration of the issues of labour market regulation and manufacturing strategy in the UK in Labour's second term. Throughout the 1980s and 1990s there remained a dominant assumption within the leadership of the Labour Party that its political failures were primarily of economic origin. The perception that the party was economically incompetent was ascribed first to its association with strategies of failed industrial intervention and the notion that it propped up an economically inefficient, unreformed public sector. Secondly, and related to the first point, was the idea that it was too closely linked to the trade union movement and associated with periods of industrial militancy. Thirdly, there was a perception that it remained an out-of-date 'tax and spend' party, unable and unwilling to adapt to the new orthodoxies championed by successive Tory governments with their tax cutting agendas and preoccupations with monetary policy over demand management.

3.5 Due to this analysis, successive defeats, especially in 1992, pushed party policy further toward a 'Supply-Side Socialism'. In doing so, it embraced the prevailing economic policy orthodoxy, accepting the view that the market economy is essentially stable, and that government intervention should be limited to ensuring the market works effectively. On this basis, the main role for government economic policy is in correcting supply-side market failures due to informational deficiencies or abuse of market power, in order to foster growth. This developing economics sought to neutralise previous criticisms and became a dominant theme of the 1997 manifesto and general strategy of political modernisation. Within this the concept of the 'New Economy' (or the 'New Knowledge Based Economy') codified policy shifts over some 18 years and forged them into a new political and economic world view underscoring much of the New Labour project. This ideological shift accounts for the 'light touch' strategy developed by the government regarding labour market regulation since 1997.

## The future of work?

3.6 Globalisation and the information and communication technologies are widely cited as the key contemporary levers of change in work and employment relations, but their apparent effects in reshaping the labour markets of the 21st century do not command a consensus. Some analysts conjure up a haunting spectre of disappearing employment opportunities in the traditional sectors of the economy, and point to growing insecurities, widening social divisions and mass unemployment. One vision is apocalyptic. 'The industrial worker', it is argued, 'is being phased out of the industrial process. While the unskilled and semi-skilled continue to be cut by the introduction of new information and communication technologies, other positions within the hierarchies are also being threatened with extinction'.[1] Others acknowledge that these changes in work systems may prompt significant developments in employment patterns in the future, but also anticipate important continuities in, for example, the service sector that accounts for the vast majority of paid jobs in advanced economies.

3.7 From a UK perspective Leadbeater is optimistic about the prospects for working life in the 21st century. Echoing earlier accounts he argues that the wider application of 'smart' technologies and the forces of globalisation are inducing the emergence of a knowledge-driven economy centred on the exploitation of intangible assets. 'The real wealth-creating economy is de-materialising,' he writes. 'The private and public sectors are increasingly using the same sorts of intangible assets – people, knowledge, ideas, information – to generate intangible outputs, services and know-how'. The consolidation of the 'New Economy' will, according to Leadbeater, 'have far-reaching consequences for the way we work, and how organisations are managed and owned'.[2] The hierarchical structures

1  N Crafts and S Broadberry, 'Explaining Anglo-American productivity differences in the mid-twentieth century' (1990) 52 *Oxford Review of Economics and Statistics* 375.
2  C Leadbeater, *Living on Thin Air: The New Economy* (2000).

and internal labour markets that characterised large public and private sector organisations are being supplanted in the new economy by networks of independent, small-scale companies based on cellular, self-managed teams.

3.8 Leadbeater's vision, dismissive of established employment patterns, is controversial. His description of work relations under the 'New Economy' recalls earlier predictions that the once dominant Fordist command and control systems of management are a major impediment to competitive success in the more flexible and global markets that characterise contemporary economic transactions. Trade unions and other allegedly rigid institutions must adapt or die, for there is no place in the 'New Economy' for traditional, adversarial industrial relations. With networks supplanting hierarchy, conflicts between worker and boss will become a distant memory. Future economic prosperity will be driven by the expanding production of knowledge and intangible assets, set against the steady erosion of traditional manufacturing and heavy industry. These commentators assume a rapid growth in scientific, technical, managerial and professional employment and a corresponding decline in traditional manual work.

3.9 In this vision, the distinction between worker and employer is withering away as the wage-labour system is consigned to history. For elements within the Labour Party this ideological analysis of the world of work functionally resolves the historical dilemma inherent in previous Labour governments' support for manufacturing, given the assumption that support for this sector offers diminishing returns. It reinforces intellectually an in-built hostility to organised labour and labour market regulation from some of those within the Labour government, and explains the failure adequately to address the legacy of a de-regulated employment law inherited from the Conservative governments. Their relevance belongs to an obsolete, conflictual industrial era. Economic policy becomes re-focused on market (and government) failure in the provision of human capital – captured in the famous focus on 'education, education, education'. Concessions to labour market regulation have to be forced out of the government and are seen as residual trade-offs to appease 'Old Labour' – an out-dated hangover from the 'Old Economy'.

## Changing labour markets in Britain

3.10 The approach of 'New Economy' pundits is nothing less than a justification for old-fashioned labour market regulation in which workers and trade unions have few rights. A tendency in much recent writing is to postulate universal or dominant trends as a consequence of radical shifts in technology or globalisation, but the changes taking place in labour markets and work patterns are typically more piecemeal, uneven and contradictory. Too often substituting anecdote or assertion for analysis, 'New Economy-ists' tend to ignore the empirical record. Highlighting recent developments in the structure of employment, occupations, unemployment and economic inactivity, some of the key claims are subjected to scrutiny below, focussing on employment restructuring and occupational change.

## Employment restructuring

3.11 It is certainly the case that one of the main developments in the UK's employment structure has been a decisive shift in broad sectoral terms away from agriculture, primary and manufacturing industry towards services. Manual employment has been eclipsed by non-manual occupations, yet still accounts for over 10 million employees. Since the late 1970s employment in agriculture has accounted for only one per cent of the total, whilst employment in construction and the former public utilities (gas, water and mining) dipped after the privatisation programme of the 1980s. By far the most marked changes have occurred in manufacturing and services. The falling share of manufacturing employment (the process of de-industrialisation) is common to most advanced economies, but the magnitude of decline in Britain has been especially pronounced at over 50 per cent since 1960. In contrast, service sector employment has been growing, in absolute numbers and as a share of total civilian employment, since the mid-1950s.

3.12 Within these wider shifts the changing balance between 'standard' and 'non-standard' employment is critically important. Standard employment refers to full-time dependent jobs, non-standard to part-time, temporary and self-employed workers. Temporary employment at the end of the 1990s accounted for approximately seven per cent of all employee jobs. It exhibited little growth in the 1980s, rose rapidly in the wake of the early 1990s recession, but tailed-off by the end of the decade. However, the aggregate data conceal radical shifts in particular sectors. Most striking is the expansion of short, fixed-term contracts in the public services, particularly in health and education, which began in the early 1980s and accounted for over two-fifths of all temporary employment by the end of the 1990s. In the private sector, temporary working increased in most sectors during the 1990s, although often from a low base, and for the first time took root in industries such as banking and finance, previously associated with stable employment and 'jobs for life'.

3.13 Trends in temporary work thus do not support the view that the nature of jobs is changing radically. The same is true of self-employment which grew most rapidly during the early 1980s recession. Numbers rose sharply from just over seven per cent of total employment in 1979 to around 11 per cent by 1984, and continued a slow rise for the remainder of that decade. The recovery in the share of self-employment following the 1990s recession has not been sustained, however, with absolute and relative falls since 1997, particularly in the construction sector which has traditionally had a high incidence of such employment. The predictions of a steep rise in self-employment under the 'New Economy' may yet be fulfilled, but the available evidence reveals little support for such claims at the present time. The only evidence of real, sustained and unequivocal change at the present time is in relation to part-time work where the growth has been striking.

3.14 In 1971 one in six employees worked part-time. Now, with over six million part-timers, this ratio has risen to one in four. From 1979 to 1999 the number of full-time employees fell by over two million, a fall most keenly felt by male workers in manual occupations. In one in four private sector workplaces more than half the workforce now work part-time; for the public sector the figure is closer to one in three. In the private sector the share of part-time employment is particularly high in wholesale and retail (47 per cent), and hotels and catering (47 per cent); in the public services it features prominently in community services (36 per cent), health (44 per cent) and education (40 per cent). Overwhelmingly filled by women, these jobs are much more likely to be poorly paid, low-skilled and unstable with many of short hours duration. Although part-time work has risen, the 1960s saw its most rapid phase of expansion[3], and recent growth is at least as much concerned with patterns of 'poor' work as with the portfolio careers anticipated by proponents of the 'New Economy'.

## Occupational changes

3.15 With a record of continuous employment growth since 1992, the UK provides a good test of the contention that paid employment is moving decisively away from low-value production and service activities towards new knowledge-intensive sectors engaged in the production of 'intangible assets' as proposed by advocates of the 'New Economy'. Dividing the working population

---

3  J Rifkin, *The End of Work: The Decline of the Global Labour Force and the Dawn of the Post-Market Era* (1995).

into three broad groupings – 'white collar', 'traditional services' and 'craft, operative and labouring' – it is possible to discern the nature of recent trends (table 1). In line with the proponents of the 'New Economy' thesis 'white collar' workers have increased their share of total employment from 35 per cent to 37 per cent, whilst the share of traditional manual workers in manufacturing and construction has declined. Nevertheless, to draw from these aggregate figures the conclusion that the 'Old Economy' is in retreat and that future employment patterns will be driven by the expansion of the 'New Economy' would be misleading for a number of reasons.

**Table 1: Occupational changes in the 1990s**
**(employees and self-employed, including second jobs, UK)**

|  | 1992 | 1999 | Absolute change ('000s) | Compound growth 92-99 |
|---|---|---|---|---|
| 'White collar' (managers, professionals, associate professionals) | 34.6 | 37.2 | 1,520 | 2.2 |
| 'Traditional' services (clerical & secretarial, personal and protective, sales, postal, cleaning) | 40.0 | 40.7 | 1,110 | 1.5 |
| Craft, operative & labouring (manual manufacturing and construction workers) | 25.4 | 22.2 | -320 | -0.7 |
| Total employment ('000s) | 26,100 | 28,500 | 2,310 | 1.2 |

*Source:* Labour Force Survey

3.16 In the first place, the growing share of managerial and professional employment in part reflects nationally specific definitions which in the British case have a distorting and exaggerating effect. Managers of shops are classified as 'sales' workers in the US, but are treated as 'managers' in the UK. Germany and Japan include only senior managers, whereas the UK classification includes many managerial and administrative jobs that elsewhere would be defined as 'clerical' occupations. It is also the case that a significant proportion of the increasing share of managerial and professional workers is associated with developments in the public sector. True, there have been large absolute increases in the 'new' sectors such as computer systems managers (62,000), software engineers (109,000) and computer programmers (92,000). But there has been little or no growth in science-related occupations, and any increases are eclipsed by the expansion of public sector professional groups in education, health and welfare, that account for two in every five (approx. 520,000) of the extra 'white collar' employees.

3.17 Closer scrutiny shows that, in terms of absolute employment growth since 1992, the fastest growing occupations have been in four long-established services (sales assistants, data input clerks, storekeepers and receptionists); state dominated education and health services; and the caring occupations (care assistants, welfare and community workers, nursery nurses). In short, employment growth has been concentrated in occupations that could scarcely be judged new, still less the fulcrum of a 'New Economy'. Looking back on this debate about the balance between the 'Old' and the 'New' Economy, students in the future may well see the irony that the fastest growing occupation in the UK in the 1990s was hairdressing. To put it gently, there is thus a tendency to overplay the significance of occupational change, and to fail adequately to take full account of the economy as it is, and the needs of workers which it generates. The 'New Economy' may be a vision of the future but it is not yet one which is clearly in focus, in this as in other respects.

## Flexible labour markets

3.18 If a policy of 'light touch' labour market regulation is not justified in terms of the emergence of a 'New Economy', are there other grounds to justify such a stance? Did the radical reforms introduced by successive Conservative governments during the 1980s and 1990s succeed in increasing flexibility, labour mobility and access to paid employment? The erosion of trade union power and the other measures intended to deregulate labour markets were judged essential to secure the gains in performance that had eluded governments in the 1960s and 1970s. Orthodox economic theory provides unqualified support for policies that rid markets of institutional 'rigidities' and many leading economists endorsed the measures that were enacted and which now enjoy a broad political consensus. Comparing developments during the recovery from the 1990s recession with those of a decade earlier allows an assessment to be made of labour market performance before and after the 1980s changes to trade union and employment law.

3.19 The recorded changes in the level of unemployment appear to support the advocates of measures to enhance labour market flexibility. The lag between output recovery and falling claimant unemployment shortened considerably to six months from five years, whilst employment also began to grow much sooner. But a closer examination of the trends reveals a rather less impressive record and three areas of particular concern. First, the expansion of employment in response to economic recovery was weaker in the 1990s than the 1980s. The growth rates achieved were half that of the 1980s, despite only marginally lower output growth. Secondly, as noted above, employment growth in the 1990s was dominated by part-time and temporary jobs, especially in the early years of recovery. Thirdly, and worryingly, there was a significant rise in the 1990s in the number of people who would otherwise be unemployed withdrawing from the labour market altogether.

3.20 The dominant reason for rising rates of inactivity is the increasing incidence of long-term sickness among men. By the end of 2001 the number of people of working age claiming sickness related benefits had risen to over three million (one in 12 of the working-age population). Much of this growth occurred in the early 1990s, when the numbers claiming invalidity benefit alone increased by 50 per cent with the rises geographically concentrated in the old industrial regions. Yet it is scarely credible that there has been such a large increase in illness. Rather, these patterns reflect the erosion of the UK's industrial base in the 1980s, and the failure of the service sector to provide alternative employment in areas most in need. Despite the long-term downward multiplier effects set in train by industrial decline, the government remains resistant to developing appropriate industrial and regional policy, relying instead on the supply-side policy of labour market flexibility and enhancing 'employability' to restore jobs to these communities.

# Britain and the international division of labour

3.21 Britain emerged from the Second World War as the leading industrial nation in Europe, yet by the early 1960s was manifestly under-performing across a range of critical indicators. The symptoms of decline were most apparent in manufacturing. Since 1960 the share of manufacturing employment has halved – a decline far worse than that experienced by comparative western market economies. Manufacturing output and employment changes have been conditioned by internal weaknesses (lack of investment and competitiveness) and by adverse shifts in the patterns of demand. On the one hand, the pattern of domestic demand has shifted in favour of commodities produced overseas; on the other hand, manufacturers located in Britain have experienced increasing difficulties in maintaining their share of international markets. Britain became a net importer of manufactures for the first time in its history in 1983 and by 1998 its share of world trade in manufactures had slumped to below eight per cent of the total.

3.22 As early as the 1960s, Britain had become a centre for relatively cheap labour. Taking total hourly labour costs, which are derived from summing total hourly earnings and social charges (national insurance, holiday and sick pay), the UK is now well down the international league table. After the Second World War Britain was a relatively high wage economy, but by 1970 only Japan had lower labour costs than Britain. Since then the gap has narrowed between Britain and the USA but not with France, Japan and Germany (table 2).

**Table 2: Hourly labour costs in manufacturing 1960-2000**

|          | *1960* | *1970* | *1980* | *1987* | *1990* | *2000* |
|----------|--------|--------|--------|--------|--------|--------|
| UK       | 100    | 100    | 100    | 100    | 100    | 100    |
| USA      | 296    | 250    | 131    | 149    | 118    | 125    |
| Japan    | 30     | 57     | 73     | 119    | 101    | 139    |
| France   | 94     | 105    | 118    | 136    | 122    | 104    |
| Germany* | 98     | 144    | 162    | 187    | 173    | 151    |

*\* Data refer to former West Germany*

*Costs are for production workers, compared at current exchange rates.*
*Index, UK=100*

*Sources: Figures for 1960 and 1970, G Ray, 'Labour costs and international competitiveness' (1972) 61 National Institute Economic Review 53; other years Bureau of Labor Statistics (2001).*

At the same time the evidence demonstrates a substantial and enduring shortfall in productivity levels in Britain as compared to the United States, Japan and the leading West European countries. The differential with the United States opened up early on in the 20th century, and, while the extent of the gap varies significantly across industries, it has been estimated to be as high as 100 per cent in some cases[4]. The gap with workers in Europe developed much later, in the 1950s and 1960s, as other countries achieved much higher productivity growth rates following post-war reconstruction. By the 1970s these shortfalls had become entrenched (table 3).

3.23 A decade of poor, often negative annual rates of productivity growth in the 1970s was followed by more rapid advances in the 1980s. Yet this should not be seen as a vindication of the de-regulation pushed by the Thatcher governments in the 1980s, which encouraged firms to pursue the inherently limited strategy of work

4   P Robinson, *Labour Market Studies: United Kingdom* (1997)

intensification. Productivity rises in the economy as a whole, including services and primary industries, were quite modest, rising annually by only 2.3 per cent between 1979 and 1988, which was broadly in line with other leading economies. If anything, the situation has deteriorated in the 1990s. The result, as far as cost competitiveness is concerned, is to leave industries in Britain at a substantial disadvantage. Unit labour costs – total labour costs divided by the productivity of labour – are relatively high despite Britain's low labour costs. Nor is this a problem limited to manufacturing: in the service industries significant productivity shortfalls exist between the UK and the US (38 per cent), the UK and Germany (34 per cent) and the UK and France (36 per cent).

**Table 3: Relative labour productivity levels in manufacturing (GDP per hour worked)**

|         | 1950 | 1960 | 1970 | 1980 | 1987 | 1990 | 2000 |
|---------|------|------|------|------|------|------|------|
| UK      | 100  | 100  | 100  | 100  | 100  | 100  | 100  |
| USA     | 248  | 218  | 196  | 190  | 172  | 158  | 181  |
| Japan   | 28   | 43   | 85   | 124  | 116  | 128  | 128  |
| France  | 88   | 109  | 140  | 167  | 146  | 145  | 168  |
| Germany | 71   | 126  | 153  | 180  | 142  | 138  | 159  |
| Sweden  | 109  | 120  | 170  | 187  | 151  | 142  | 172  |

*Source: ICOP Industry Database, Summary Tables (www.eco.rug.nl/GGDC/icop.html)*

# Conclusion

3.24 The British economy's place in the international division of labour has been associated in recent decades with the development and consolidation of particular weaknesses. A long-standing and seemingly unbreakable record of low productivity has coincided in many industries with a history of low relative wages and inferior skills. It appears that these long-established characteristics are being reflected and reproduced in contemporary employment patterns by the expansion of relatively routine and poorly-paid jobs in the service economy. The Thatcher governments' strategy of de-regulation through the 1980s, rather than resolve the UK's economic problems, compounded many of its structural weaknesses by consolidating these moves toward comparatively low-wage, low-skilled production.

3.25 The present Labour government has argued for minimal labour market regulation due to its preoccupations with a stylised vision of the world of work associated with the futurology of the 'New Economy'. This policy stance hinges crucially on whether there is compelling evidence to support claims that the labour markets and employment patterns of the future will be radically different from the past. The data reviewed here point to shifts in employment but also important lines of continuity. The proportion of the workforce engaged in the professions, scientific and technical occupations may have increased slightly, but over the same period the total number of manual workers has been remarkably stable at around 10.5 million or 40 per cent of total employment. Add to this figure other long-standing service jobs, for example clerical and secretarial work, and the size of the traditional labour force soars to 15 million. The fastest-growing occupations include software engineers and management and business consultants, but also shelf-fillers, nursery nurses, housekeepers and prison officers.

3.26 The 'New Economy' may yet surface and succeed in transforming the future world of work, but the present structure of employment points to the emergence of an 'hour glass' economy. At the top end of the jobs hierarchy there has been an increase in high-paid jobs, whose incumbents enjoy substantial discretion over the hours, places and patterns of their working time. But in Britain their fortunes have merely served to fuel the growth of low-paid, routine and un-skilled employment in occupations that would have been pre-eminent 50 years ago. The government has recently conceded that in its first term it became preoccupied with the 'New Economy' and the labour market that operates at the top of this hour glass. If there is to be a re-focus on the majority at the bottom of the hour glass then the regulations and rights for people at work discussed in the following pages must move centre stage in terms of the policy agenda of the government. This is not just because a modern society should do no less than provide such minimal rights for people at work. They are also necessary to boost our productive capacity.

# Chapter 4

# Social justice and employment rights

4.1 Employment provides workers with an income and is crucial in defining a worker's living standards; it is also an important influence over the status and advancement of workers and their families, as well as the quality of their wider social life. Access to employment, the treatment of workers within it, and their related ability to remain employed are therefore all of central importance to the role that work plays in enhancing social justice. This chapter considers four areas of employment regulation: the national minimum wage, working time, training, and occupational health and safety.

## The national minimum wage: from a minimum wage to a fair wage

4.2 The national minimum wage is now firmly established as part of the framework of employment rights of British workers. The main rate was originally set in April 1999 at £3.60 per hour. But following increases in both 2000 and 2001, it stood at £4.10 in October 2001, and has been recommended by the Low Pay Commission to increase further to £4.20 in October 2002. Yet while this rate applies to the vast majority of workers, the government has used its power (a) to set different rates in certain circumstances to exclude some workers, and (b) to set a lower so-called 'development' rate for younger workers and workers in receipt of specified training. This is currently £3.50 per hour and has been recommended to increase to £3.60 from October 2002 by the Low Pay Commission. At the time of its introduction, opponents of the national minimum wage predicted that it would have dire economic and social consequences.

But these predictions have proved to be ill-judged, and the national minimum wage has already made a real contribution to achieving greater social justice for the low paid. Nevertheless, certain problems do exist with the current national minimum wage system as a means of protecting the position of low paid workers.

## Exclusions and differential wage rates

4.3 The government was admirably resistant to most special pleading for exemptions from the national minimum wage. But it did not resist all such pleading. Workers aged 16 or 17 at present have no national minimum wage entitlement. This exclusion, which reflects the State's policy to encourage this age group to either stay in education or be in receipt of some form of vocational training, therefore leaves open the potential for such workers to be employed on very low pay rates and then to be replaced with younger workers once they have become entitled to the national minimum wage. Moreover, the lower national wage rate set for workers aged 18-21 inclusive might have been justified initially as a wise precaution in case the introduction of the national minimum wage had a marked adverse impact on the employment experience of younger workers. But the evidence points to 18 rather than 21 – let alone 22 – as being the age when full adult rates are paid in most jobs. Consequently, the present arrangements would seem to be out of line with labour market practice and therefore unnecessary. Furthermore, the evidence does not support the concern that payment of the full national minimum wage rate to all workers at 18 would have adverse consequences for the employment of younger workers.

4.4 The provision of the same low wage rate for workers in receipt of what is, in effect, specified day release training for 26 weeks, is equally questionable since it has evidently not provided an incentive for employers to require or encourage workers to use this route to attain new skills. Similarly, the exclusion of apprentices from any national minimum wage entitlement in the first year of their apprenticeship has not been shown to have led to any growth in this route to skilled jobs. The current patchwork of exclusions and lower rates therefore needs a radical rethink in order to give greater credence to the national minimum wage as a universal entitlement. The lower rate provided for 18-21 year olds is out of step with labour market practice and the available evidence does not suggest that the 'training rate' has provided an effective incentive to employers to use the designated training arrangements to enhance the skills of their workforces. Furthermore, the complete exclusion of 16 and 17 year olds, as well as first year apprentices, lacks any credible justification.

Indeed, the Low Pay Commission itself has argued that a rate for 16 and 17 year old workers should be positively considered.

## Enforcement

4.5 There are currently two different ways of enforcement of the national minimum wage. First, there is a range of individual rights for workers: to claim any shortfall in pay below the national minimum wage as an unlawful deduction in an employment tribunal or as a contractual right in the county court; to access the (rather limited) national minimum wage records that employers are required to keep, accompanied by another person of their choice; and to seek redress for any detriment or dismissal that occurs because they try to enforce their relevant statutory rights. Second, enforcement officers – a role given by the government to the Inland Revenue, which has designated certain officers for this purpose – are accorded a number of enforcement rights. These are to access employers' records, to bring proceedings to enforce payment of the national minimum wage to identified workers, and to issue 'enforcement' and 'penalty' notices requiring employers to pay the requisite rates, the sanction for non-compliance with a penalty notice being a financial penalty of twice the current national minimum wage rate per worker per day of non-compliance.

4.6 Notwithstanding these arrangements, enforcement has emerged as the main problem with the current regulatory framework. This is because a major disjunction exists between the substantive rights provided to workers and the powers that Revenue enforcement officers possess to ensure that these rights are actually provided. Observance of the national minimum wage by low paying employers depends primarily on effective action by these enforcement officers. The Revenue, in pursuance of this enforcement role, has set up an admirably accessible system for seeking its assistance via a telephone hotline or internet link and there is broad agreement that its officers discharge their duties with appropriate firmness and concern. But while the Revenue can secure payments to those who have been underpaid, it cannot take any action to protect those workers against the adverse consequences that employers may visit on them by way of reprisal. This lack of enforcement power is, furthermore, compounded by the fact that low paid workers are the least likely to have either the capacity or economic freedom to invoke their rights to complain that they have suffered a detriment or been dismissed in such circumstances. In practice, they frequently have no effective means of protection against any retaliatory action taken by their employer.

4.7 Low paid workers consequently need greater access to third party help to secure all their national minimum wage rights – pay at the specified rate without the risk of discrimination or loss of their job. Although these are workers who badly need trade union help, they are also among the least likely to be union members. At the same time, it is quite widely acknowledged that there are limits to the enforcement functions which the Inland Revenue could appropriately be expected to exercise. An alternative solution would be the revival of a labour inspectorate. Such an inspectorate could be provided with powers extensive enough to enable it to enforce the minimum wage in a manner which pre-empts the risk of detriment to workers who take to the initiative to secure the payment of their statutory rights. The labour inspectorate would replace the enforcement functions of the Inland Revenue, and ought to be part of a general rethink in terms of what can be done to ensure that the employment rights provided to workers generally become a reality for those they are intended to benefit. The role of the labour inspectorate would thus extend beyond enforcing the minimum wage, and some of these additional responsibilities are considered in chapter 9.

## Raising the standard: fair pay not a minimum wage

4.8 To date, the government has set the national minimum wage at the 'prudent' rates recommended by the Low Pay Commission (with some qualifications and exceptions). Trade union and other evidence to the Commission has made the case for the rate to be set at a higher level in real terms and this case is undoubtedly a strong one. Indeed the case is strengthened by obligations under international law. By article 4 of the Council of Europe's Social Charter of 18 October 1961, the United Kingdom has undertaken to 'recognise the right of workers to a remuneration such as will give them and their families a decent standard of living'. The Social Rights Committee of the Council of Europe has concluded that this means that the minimum wage should be set at 60 per cent of the national average male rate. This obligation should be the target rate for the minimum wage.

4.9 But although there is a compelling case for raising the level of the minimum wage, there is also a wider perspective to be born in mind here in relation to the issue of what minimum pay entitlements should be provided to workers. In the past, minimum wage fixing has also embraced the concept of a 'fair wage'. While this is more difficult to translate into a legal right, there are precedents in the quasi-legal 'fair wages' regime established by the Fair Wages Resolutions of the House of Commons from 1891-1983 and related 'fair wages legislation' which made certain licences or subsidies conditional, *inter alia*, on observance of wages which were at least as good as the norm for the relevant job. There is consequently scope for rethinking this 'rate for the job' concept of fair wages, linked to occupational, sectoral, and/or area norms: this ought to be a second tier protection above the absolute floor fixed by the national minimum wage. Indeed, there is an arguable case that a worker's right to decent pay should embrace both the right to a national statutory minimum and the right to a 'fair wage' established by an appropriate form of reference to prevailing normal practice.

## Recommendations

i *Entitlement to the national minimum wage should be extended to all workers, regardless of their age or whether they are in the first year of an apprenticeship. In addition, the current development rate for 18-21 year olds should be abolished.*

ii *A labour inspectorate should be created, with responsibilities to include enforcement of the national minimum wage and the protection of workers who seek to enforce their statutory rights.*

iii *The national minimum wage should be based on the European decency threshold, 60 per cent of the national average male wage.*

iv *Provision should be made for a 'second tier' protection for workers through the provision of a right to receive a 'fair wage' established by reference to an appropriate form of reference to prevailing 'normal practice'.*

v *The standard reference point for a 'fair wage' should be appropriate collective agreements and the general level of pay applying in the industry in question.*

# Working time

4.10 Historically working time in Britain has been the subject of little legal regulation, and successive Conservative governments from 1979 onwards removed most of the statutory protections that did exist. The introduction of the Working Time Regulations 1998, in order to implement the EC Working Time Directive, therefore heralded a new and positive regulatory framework. This provided the following *basic* rights:

- a maximum average working week for all 'workers' of 48 hours, *including overtime*, normally calculated over a 17-week reference period;
- a maximum average of eight hours' work in each 24-hour period for 'night workers';
- free health assessments for both existing night workers and those being assigned to night work;

- a minimum daily rest period of 11 consecutive hours;
- a minimum weekly rest period of at least 24 hours (or 48 hours in any two week period);
- a 20 minutes rest break for any adult worker whose daily working time exceeds six and a half hours and a corresponding one for young workers after four and a half hours; and
- four weeks' paid annual leave.

The government adopted a minimalist approach towards the transposition of the directive. As a consequence, the Working Time Regulations suffer from a number of serious deficiencies that go a long way to explain why, in a country where average weekly working hours are the longest in the European Union, the number of workers and the proportion of the workforce regularly working in excess of 48 hours a week both *rose* between 1992 and 2001.

## The individual opt-out

4.11 An individual worker may at present expressly agree in writing to opt out of the 48-hour maximum working week laid down in regulation 4 of the Working Time Regulations and thereby work longer hours. This opt out, while permissible under the working time directive, is clearly undesirable in a measure that is intended to avoid excessive working hours. It is even more so given that employers, as a result of a recent amendment to the 1998 regulations, do not any longer have to record the number of hours worked by those who have exercised their 'right' to opt out, but simply need to keep a list of them. Furthermore workers may be subjected to great pressure to agree to exercise this 'right' of opt out, and there are no protections in the form of a requirement that the worker must first seek independent advice before exercising this 'right'. Low pay may be another factor which induces workers to 'agree' to exercise their 'right' to opt out, which is another reason for addressing the level of the minimum wage and instituting a fair wage procedure. Britain is the only country to have taken advantage of the 'right' of individual opt out. It should be revoked.

## Definition of 'working time'

4.12 'Working time' under the 1998 Regulations is defined as 'any period during which [a worker] is working, at his employer's disposal and carrying out his activities'. This definition is, for the most part, unproblematic. However, following a European Court of Justice ruling, it appears only to cover 'on-call' time when either (a) workers are required to be physically present at their workplace, even if not actually working; or (b) where they are based at the workplace and are actually carrying out work duties. It therefore seems that workers can be in a situation where on-call hours do not count as working time, even when their freedom to engage in non-work activities is circumscribed, perhaps geographically by the need to be 'contactable'. Another problem with the 1998 regulations concerns how a worker's normal working hours is calculated for the purposes of applying the restriction imposed with regard to the average length of night work. Under the regulations only contractually *guaranteed* overtime counts (that is, overtime that an employee is obliged to work *and* which the employer is obliged to offer). Other types of overtime (whether wholly voluntary or under a contractual term that binds *only* the employee) are therefore not counted towards the eight-hour average.

## Partially unmeasured working time

4.13 The working time directive provides for the possibility of derogating from its requirements when 'on account of the specific characteristics of the activity concerned, the duration of the working time is not measured and/or predetermined or can be determined by workers themselves'. It gives the following particular examples of workers who may be covered by this derogation: managing executives or 'other persons with autonomous decision-taking powers'; family workers; and workers officiating at religious ceremonies in churches and religious communities. These provisions are reproduced in the 1998 regulations, and effectively remove many workers from the limits on working time laid down in the directive. In 1999 a new regulation 20(2) extended the scope of this derogation to cover workers who, in the words of the government, have some, but not all, of their working time pre-determined (for example, by contract) and choose to work longer of their own volition. This new provision offers employers the clear opportunity to apply 'subtle pressure' to skilled, professional and managerial staff to work longer hours. The 1999 amendment is a further erosion of the limited protection in the directive.

## Workforce agreements

4.14 Under the Working Time Regulations the provisions on night work and daily and weekly rest breaks for adult workers can be modified or excluded by virtue of a collective agreement with an independent trade union or by a 'workforce agreement'. Workers to whom such agreements apply must receive an equivalent period of compensatory rest or, if that is not possible, other appropriate protection for their health and safety. Furthermore, agreements of this type can also be used to increase the reference period for averaging the maximum working week to up to 52 weeks in certain circumstances. These provisions are perhaps acceptable insofar as they relate to agreements concluded between employers and independent trade unions. In other situations, however, they provide employers with an opportunity to circumvent the statutory safeguards by engaging in negotiations with specially elected worker's representatives who may have neither the training nor expertise to bargain effectively; or, in the case of workplaces with 20 or fewer employees, pressurising the majority of the workforce to agree to their demands. The qualification of statutory rights should be subject to the most stringent requirements, and it should not be possible for an agreement of this kind to be made unless with a recognised trade union, failing which an Information and Consultative body set up under the Information and Consultation Directive once it has been introduced into British law.

## Enforcement

4.15 A final matter that is a significant concern with regard to the current regulatory framework relates to the arrangements put in place for enforcing the 1998 regulations. These arrangements embody two different enforcement mechanisms which are linked to the distinction that the regulations draw between the working time '*limits*' they impose, and the '*entitlements*' that they provide to rest breaks, daily and weekly rest periods, and holidays. With regard to working time limits, specific obligations are imposed on employers 'to take all reasonable steps' to *ensure* compliance with those laid down in respect of weekly working time and night working. Non-compliance with these obligations can be addressed by health and safety inspectors, although it is worth noting that in 2000/2001 the Health and Safety Executive issued only 14 improvement notices relating to the working time regulations. In contrast, there is no positive obligation on employers to provide 'entitlements', although workers have a right to complain to an employment tribunal if they are not received. As a result, providing that an employer makes *provision* for rest breaks, rest periods and holidays, workers may choose whether or not to take them. In this sense they are therefore 'voluntary', which means that, if a worker has opted out of the 48-hour maximum average working week, he or she could in theory work 24 hours a day, 365 days year.

### Recommendations

*vi*    *The current ability of employers to secure the agreement of workers to opt out of the 48 hour maximum working week should be revoked. Workers are generally not permitted to 'agree' to work in conditions which present a danger to their health and safety. Working time should not be an exception to this rule.*

vii *Legislative action should be taken to ensure that working time includes any periods during which the non-work lives of workers are disrupted by on-call or similar arrangements. 'Normal working hours' for the purposes of the Working Time Regulations should be redefined so that they extend to encompass all overtime working, regardless of whether or not it is contractually guaranteed.*

viii *The exclusion of workers whose duration of working time is not measured and/or predetermined or is determined by workers themselves should be applied as narrowly as possible. The Working Time Regulations should be amended accordingly, and the extension of the exclusion by regulation 20(2) introduced in 1999 should be revoked.*

ix *Any modification of workers' rights under the Working Time Regulations should be permissible only by a collective agreement with an independent trade union, failing which a standing representative body of employees established under the Information and Consultation Directive, once implemented.*

x *Employers should be obliged to ensure compliance with the current regulatory requirements on the provision of rest breaks, rest periods and holidays. More effective enforcement mechanisms should be developed; enforcement of the Working Time Regulations should be the responsibility of the proposed labour inspectorate.*

## Training and development

4.16 The institutional framework relating to training has undergone repeated and radical changes over the last three decades. The Industrial Training Act 1964 established a national system of industrial training boards which contained representatives of both employers and unions and were funded by payroll levies on the former. In the 1980s, this system was dismantled and replaced by employer-dominated Training and Enterprise Councils that were financed by a combination of state funding and individual income generation. Recently, these councils have themselves been abolished, and replaced by a system of national and local learning and skills councils operating under the umbrella of a Sector Skills Council Development Agency. In addition, these latter developments have been accompanied by a bewildering range of other initiatives introduced or proposed, aimed at improving the training performance of the British economy. These include:

- the provision of training opportunities to certain categories of the unemployed under the New Deal Programme;
- the creation of a University for Industry which is intended to stimulate the demand for lifelong learning among individuals and businesses;
- proposed pilot schemes providing paid education leave to those without basic skills and/or NVQ level 2 qualifications;
- significant changes to the modern apprenticeship system;
- major reforms to 14-19 year old education;
- establishment of a union learning fund that seeks to support unions in promoting learning at work; and
- a right for recognised unions to appoint 'Learning Representatives' who will be entitled to receive paid time off to receive training and undertake a number of statutory functions, including analysing learning and training needs, providing information and advice on training and learning, and consulting with employers.

## Britain's poor training record

4.17 The British training system is thus a highly complex and rapidly changing one. At the same time, international comparisons of training activity have continually revealed that Britain's track record is poor. Indeed, the available evidence indicates that only a minority of employees receive any training in a given year and that much of the training which is provided is often focused on managerial personnel. It also indicates, according to the CBI and the TUC, in a joint submission to the government's Productivity Initiative, that:

- about seven million adults, one in five of adults of working age, have low levels of literacy and numeracy;
- almost nine million people, 32 per cent of the workforce, are not qualified to NVQ Level 2 (equivalent to 5 GCSEs at grades A*-C);
- low skilled workers receive less training than highly skilled workers; and
- part-time workers have less training than full-time or temporary employees.

4.18 Two main explanations have been put forward to explain the poor training record of British employers. The first links it to a variety of institutional factors, such as short-termism in capital markets, low state intervention, and a lack of collective organisation on the part of employers and unions, that have acted to encourage companies to pursue a low-cost and low-skill product market strategies. The second, focuses attention on failures in the 'training market' that have led to a low demand for training from both individual workers and employers. In the case of individuals, this low level of demand has been attributed to a lack of knowledge about opportunities and a lack of resources to take advantage of them. In the case of employers, it has been linked to doubts about the potential returns on training expenditure that stem, in part, from fears that trained staff will be poached by other employers, fears that have further been seen to explain the reluctance of employers to invest in 'generic', as opposed to firm-specific, skills.

## Strategies for reform

4.19 In combination, these explanations suggest that Britain's poor training record cannot be effectively challenged in the absence of wider governmental policies aimed at reversing the low skills-low cost strategies of employers. They also suggest that it is highly unlikely that the nature and level of training can be significantly increased through a voluntaristic approach to reform that does not effectively challenge the short-termism that all too often informs current employer attitudes towards investment in workforce skills and competencies. Given this, there would seem to be a clear need for much stronger forms of government intervention that encompass legislative reforms aimed at addressing three, inevitably inter-related, features of the current training system:

- the lack of information and support provided to individual workers;
- the lack of collective and joint ownership of training on the part of trade unions and employers' organisations that would serve to reinforce the greater conceptualisation of training as a long-term 'collective good';
- the absence of mechanisms which ensure that employers adequately invest in workforce training.

## Worker support

4.20 At present, workers' rights to receive training are extremely limited. In fact, a major weakness of the current national arrangements is that they not only leave employers free to decide how much money to expend on training, but also place an onus on individual workers to pursue their own training, largely in their own time and at their own expense. There is consequently a strong case for pursuing the logic underlying the government's recent decision to establish a series of paid educational leave pilots and provide workers with statutory rights to both receive training and to be given the paid time off that is necessary for them to undergo training. A model of how this might be done, in fact, already exists. Under section 63A of the Employment Rights Act 1996 employees who are aged 16 or 17 have the right to paid time off to undergo study or training aimed at the achievement of certain qualifications. In addition, those aged 18 years are permitted reasonable time off to obtain a relevant qualification. There seems no reason why rights of this type could not be made universal. Furthermore, the introduction of such rights could be supported by two further measures:

- the specification of some form of minimum entitlement to training, such as ten days a year, as has been suggested by the GMB;
- the provision of explicit training entitlements to workers made redundant in order that they have the opportunity to enhance their future employment prospects.

## Joint ownership

4.21 There is a clear need, as already noted, to provide workers with some collective means of participating in management training policies and priorities. At the workplace level, this could be done by providing that all recognised trade unions have a right to be consulted by employers about training, a matter to which we return in chapter 7 below. It could also be partly addressed through ensuring that the consultative mechanisms put in place in order to implement the EC Directive on Information and Consultation extend to encompass training. Other reforms that could be used to support these developments would be a requirement for employers to draw up, in conjunction with recognised unions, or in their absence, other workforce representatives established under the Information and Consultation directive when implemented, annual training plans, and for the implementation of these to be supported by an additional obligation annually to prepare development plans for individual workers. Reforms of this kind would go some way to creating some form of joint ownership over training at the organisational level. But the process of enhancing joint ownership could be further extended to encompass the establishment of sectoral training bodies that would be governed jointly by employer and union representatives.

## Employer funding

4.22 There is clearly a continuing role for government funding of training. Action, however, is needed to increase the investment made by employers. The CBI and the TUC have jointly supported the use of tax credits to support such an increase. This approach may be of value, but it would leave unchanged the present voluntaristic approach towards employer training provision that has clearly failed the economy. A more interventionist approach is therefore required. One option is to require all employers to spend a given percentage of their turnover on training, although the monitoring of compliance with this requirement is likely to be difficult. An alternative option would be to 'go back to the future' and reinstate a system of payroll levies which would be used to fund the joint sectoral training bodies discussed above. However, before moving in this direction, careful thought would need to be given to whether such a system could be designed in a way that ensures the provision of relevant and good quality training.

## Recommendations

xi *All workers should have a right to receive paid time off to undergo study or training. This right should be supported by the provision to workers of a minimum annual entitlement to training, along with the laying down of explicit training entitlements to those made redundant.*

xii *Joint controlled sectoral training bodies should be established, and more extensive rights for trade unions and workers to negotiate and be consulted over workplace training matters should be introduced, including the development of workplace and individual training plans.*

xiii *Consideration should be given to the introduction of a system of employer 'payroll' levies that could be used to fund joint employer-union sectoral level training activities.*

# Health and safety at work

4.23 The issue of workplace health and safety can be seen to encompass three distinct, but inter-related goals.

- the prevention of work-related injuries and illness;
- the provision of compensation and financial support to the victims of such harm; and
- the access of such victims to timely and appropriate rehabilitation services.

In addition to these three issues, there are two related points which arise for consideration. These relate to worker representation and participation on health and safety matters, as well as questions of enforcement.

## Prevention of injury and illness

4.24 The prevention of work-related harm is regulated by the Health and Safety at Work etc Act 1974. Yet it is clear that the Act has not served to reduce levels of work-related harm to acceptable levels. For example, the Health and Safety Executive has estimated, on the basis of self-report survey data, that around 2.8 million workers each year suffer accidents or ill health 'caused or made worse by work'. The available evidence suggests that many employers continue to accord the protection of worker health and safety a relatively low priority when compared to the importance attached to broader financial and operation considerations. Moreover, the majority of employers, particularly smaller ones, often do not have access to specialist expertise in the form of safety advisers/managers and occupational health personnel who can be used to assist in the adequate identification of risks, and in the adoption and implementation of appropriate preventive measures. On top of this, many small and medium sized employers apparently face difficulties in understanding what they need to do to comply with modern goal-orientated and non-prescriptive statutory requirements, and Health and Safety Executive commissioned research has revealed widespread employer ignorance of their legal obligations.

4.25 Reforms are needed to address each of the above weaknesses of the present law. These actions need, in turn, to be supported by others aimed at addressing significant other gaps in the coverage of the current regulatory regime. For example, there is a clear need for more explicit duties to be laid down in respect of the prevention of the two most common sources of work-related ill health, namely musculoskeletal conditions and stress/depression. Similarly, action is also needed to introduce more detailed legislative requirements concerning the steps employers should take to manage work-related transport risks; and protect the health and safety of those engaged in 'non-standard' forms of employment, such as temporary workers, homeworkers and self-employed sub-contractors.

## Worker representation and participation

4.26 A key area of weakness of the present legal framework concerns the regulatory provisions relating to worker representation and participation. Existing provisions are contained in two main sets of regulations: the Safety Representatives and Safety Committees Regulations 1977, and the Health and Safety (Consultation with Employees) Regulations 1996. The first of these regulations enables recognised unions to appoint safety representatives from amongst employees, and provide these representatives with a number of rights. These relate to such matters as the provision of paid time off to carry out their functions and undergo training, the receipt of information from employers, the carrying out of inspections and investigations, and the establishment of safety committees. The second set of regulations require employers to consult, either directly or via elected representatives, those employees not covered by union appointed safety representatives. However, representatives so elected are not provided with the same rights as their union counterparts. For example, they do not have the right to carry out workplace inspections or request the establishment of a safety committee.

4.27 Against a background of declining union membership and recognition in the 1980s and 1990s, the coverage, both in terms of workplaces and workers, of union safety representatives appointed under the Safety Representatives and Safety Committees Regulations 1977, fell substantially. This decline acted to reduce the role of one of the key mechanisms of workplace self-regulation and, given the evidence that exists which suggests that injury rates are lower in union organised workplaces, almost certainly had a detrimental impact on standards of workplace safety. Furthermore, experience shows that where union representatives do exist, they often confront problems as a result of weaknesses in their legal rights and the way in which these are enforced. For example, it has been found that representatives face difficulties in securing paid time off, frequently do not receive from employers the information they are legally entitled to, and often do not consider themselves to be adequately consulted or involved in the carrying out of the risk assessments that are required under a number of regulatory provisions. These problems clearly, in large part, stem from employer unwillingness to comply with current legal requirements. Their occurrence, however, is not helped by three other factors:

- the inability of safety representatives directly to enforce their rights, except in the area of paid time off, where there is a right of complaint to an employment tribunal;
- inspector resistance to getting involved in industrial relations issues and hence taking action to enforce the relevant statutory provisions;
- the current limitations on the ability of worker representatives to take action in cases where employers are failing in a serious way to comply with their legal duties to protect the health and safety of workers.

## Problems of enforcement

4.28 It is not, however, only in the area of worker representation and participation where problems exist with regard to the enforcement of health and safety law. Rather, this constitutes a more general problem. Between them, local authorities and the Health and Safety Executive have the equivalent of around 3,000 inspectors engaged in fieldwork activities. This is a low level of staffing which has obvious adverse implications for the likelihood of a workplace being inspected and the frequency with which such inspections occur. Indeed, on average, it is likely that each workplace can only be expected every five to six years. It is also the case that the Health and Safety Executive inspectors investigate only a small proportion of reported accidents, and they make relatively limited use of their direct enforcement powers, in the sense that only a very small proportion of inspections result in either the bringing of prosecutions or the issuing of improvement and prohibition notices. Moreover, where prosecutions are brought, prison sentences are virtually never imposed, while the fines imposed on employers are frequently low, and represent only a very small proportion of company turnover and profits.

## Compensation and financial support

4.29 At present, the provision of compensation and financial support to workers who suffer injury or ill health as a result of work activities comes from three main sources:

- various forms of employer 'benefits';
- Industrial Injuries Disablement Benefit under the Industrial Injuries Scheme; and
- compensation through fault-based personal injury litigation.

Serious problems surround each of these sources of support. As regards those provided directly by employers, workers do not have any statutory entitlements to sick pay, beyond the provision of Statutory Sick Pay of £63.25 a week for 28 weeks, and as a result have highly variable access to such income while away from work due to work-related injury or ill health. Furthermore, relatively few employers have income protection insurance under which employees receive regular payments that would provide them, in conjunction with state benefits, close to full earnings during periods when they are unable to work. In addition, rapidly increasing numbers of employees are not covered by final salary pension schemes under which they can retire early on ill health grounds and receive credit not only for accrued service but for the future service which would have been completed had they continued in employment up to the normal retirement age.

4.30 These weaknesses in employer provided financial support are compounded by serious problems with regard to the other forms of support. With regard to Industrial Injuries Disablement Benefit, this does have the virtue of being payable on a long-term and no-fault basis. Against this, the benefits provided are very low, being limited to a maximum of £114.80 per week, and entitlement only arises if the extent of the disability is assessed at 14 per cent or more. Furthermore, in the case of work-related ill health, benefits are only payable in respect of certain 'prescribed diseases', with the result that it is often not available to workers suffering from musculo-skeletal and stress-related conditions. As regards personal injury litigation, this can produce relatively large compensation awards. However, only a small proportion of those harmed at work receive compensation through it and such litigation is both costly and time consuming.

## Rehabilitation

4.31 Rehabilitation can be seen to encompass two main elements. First, the provision of medical treatment aimed at maximising recovery from physical or mental illness. Secondly, the provision of vocational services, such as functional evaluations, training, and work adaptations intended to enable workers to obtain or retain employment. Rehabilitation can therefore require contributions from a number of different types of specialists, for example, doctors, nurses, physiotherapists, occupational therapists, psychologists and ergonomists. Both the State and individual employers contribute to the provision of rehabilitation. At the level of the State, this contribution is primarily provided through medical treatment in the National Health Service and the various forms of advisory and financial support that can be obtained from the Employment Service. At the level of employers, the contribution is chiefly made by occupational health services, the provision of both private medical and income protection insurance cover, and the making of temporary or permanent workplace adjustments.

4.32 The fact remains, nevertheless, that the available support for rehabilitation to ill and injured workers compares very unfavourably with the position in other countries. As a result, all too often workers unnecessarily lose their jobs or have extended periods away from work. This is clearly unacceptable. But there is no easy solution to remedy this situation, given that the necessary remedial action will require inputs from the National Health Service, a number of government departments and agencies, and employers. That said, and drawing on the approaches of other countries, there are clear measures that could be taken to improve employer provision. One such measure would be to introduce a regulatory regime requiring employers to have access to multi-disciplinary occupational health and safety services. Others would be to require employers to appoint staff with the specific responsibility for looking after the rehabilitation of ill and injured workers, including the carrying out of any necessary liaison without outside medical services, and the development of plans aimed at supporting their return to work and continued employment.

## Recommendations

xiv    *The duties imposed on employers under the Health and Safety at Work etc. Act 1974 should be amended to: (a) detail more specifically the management, organisation and arrangements that employers need to put in place in respect of the management of health and safety at work; and (b) spell out the 'preventive principles' or objectives that should inform the development and implementation of these arrangements.*

xv     *Existing gaps in regulatory coverage should be addressed, notably by the development of new regulatory packages on such issues as the management of work transport, temporary working and sub-contracting, and the ergonomic design of work tasks and schedules. In addition, 'principles of prevention' should include the need for employers to adjust work to the physical and psychological capabilities of workers and, more generally, to protect and enhance the 'quality of working life'.*

xvi    *A system of mobile union safety representatives should be established to cover smaller workplaces, and steps should be taken to equalise the representation rights provided to union and non-union workers. In addition, the powers of workplace representatives should be extended by the introduction of rights to 'stop the job' in prescribed circumstances of danger to health and safety, issue 'Provisional Improvement Notices' where it is believed there is a serious infringement of statutory health and safety standards, and enforce all of their rights through complaints to employment tribunals.*

xvii   *There should be a substantial increase in Health and Safety Executive and local authority inspector numbers, together with the adoption of a more rigorous approach to the enforcement of health and safety laws, including a greater willingness to bring prosecutions and take cases on indictment to the Crown Court. These changes should be supported by raising the maximum levels of fines that can be imposed by magistrates, removing the current restrictions on the use of imprisonment, and the use of other penalties, such as 'proportionate fines' linked to company turnover or profits, 'equity' fines whereby fines would be paid in the form of new share capital, and 'corporate probation' orders. In addition the current manslaughter law should be changed to introduce a new offence of 'corporate killing' and facilitate the prosecution of directors who*

---

*recklessly endanger worker health and safety, along with the imposition under the Health and Safety at Work Act 1974 of an explicit health and safety duty on directors.*

xviii *Workers who are injured at work should be entitled to full sick pay for a year, and attention should be paid to the adverse consequences for workers injured at work of the current trend away from final salary pension schemes.*

xix *A more generous and extensive system of no-fault compensation should be introduced to provide injured and ill workers with long-term benefits. In addition, in order to avoid the difficulties associated with establishing the work-related nature of many health conditions, consideration should be given to making such compensation available on a 'non-work-related' basis. The introduction of an expanded and more generous no-fault compensation system should be funded by employer contributions and these contributions should be 'performance-rated'. Consideration should also be given to operating this system on a sectoral and jointly controlled basis, in order to increase the potential for it to take on a more general preventive role via the provision of guidance and advice and, perhaps, the establishment of regional occupational health and safety services that can be utilised by smaller employers.*

xx *Employers should be required to appoint 'rehabilitation coordinators' and to develop rehabilitation plans for ill and injured workers whose absence from work exceeds, or is likely to exceed, a specified length of time.*

# Conclusion

## National minimum wage

i   Entitlement to the national minimum wage should be extended to all workers, regardless of their age or whether they are in the first year of an apprenticeship. In addition, the current development rate for 18-21 year olds should be abolished.

ii   A labour inspectorate should be created, with responsibilities to include enforcement of the national minimum wage and the protection of workers who seek to enforce their statutory rights.

iii   The national minimum wage should be based on the European decency threshold, 60 per cent of the national average male wage.

iv   Provision should be made for a 'second tier' protection for workers through the provision of a right to receive a 'fair wage' established by reference to an appropriate form of reference to prevailing normal practice.

v   The standard reference points for a 'fair wage' should be appropriate collective agreements and the general level of pay applying in the industry in question.

## Working time

vi   The current ability of employers to secure the agreement of workers to opt out of the 48 hour maximum working week should be revoked. Workers are generally not permitted to 'agree' to work in conditions which present a danger to their health and safety. Working time should not be an exception to this rule.

vii   Legislative action should be taken to ensure that working time includes any periods during which the non-work lives of workers are disrupted by on-call or similar arrangements. 'Normal working hours' for the purposes of the Working Time Regulations should be redefined so that they extend to encompass all overtime working, regardless of whether or not it is contractually guaranteed.

viii   The exclusion of workers whose duration of working time is not measured and/or predetermined or is determined by workers themselves should be applied as narrowly as possible. The Working Time Regulations should be amended accordingly, and the extension of the exclusion by regulation 20(2) introduced in 1999 should be revoked.

ix Any modification of workers' rights under the Working Time Regulations should be permissible only by a collective agreement with an independent trade union, failing which a standing representative body of employees established under the Information and Consultation Directive, once implemented.

x Employers should be obliged to ensure compliance with the current regulatory requirements on the provision of rest breaks, rest periods and holidays. More effective enforcement mechanisms should be developed, and enforcement of the Working Time Regulations should be the responsibility of the proposed labour inspectorate.

## Training and development

xi All workers should have a right to receive paid time off to undergo study or training. This right should be supported by the provision to workers of a minimum annual entitlement to training, along with the laying down of explicit training entitlements to those made redundant.

xii Joint controlled sectoral training bodies should be established and more extensive rights for trade unions and workers to negotiate and be consulted over workplace training matters should be introduced, including the development of workplace and individual training plans.

xiii A system of employer 'payroll' levies should be introduced. These should be set at a level sufficient to increase aggregate levels of training, and to fund joint employer-union sectoral level training activities.

## Health and safety at work

xiv The duties imposed on employers under the Health and Safety at Work etc. Act 1974 should be amended to: (a) detail more specifically the management, organisation and arrangements that employers need to put in place in respect of the management of health and safety at work; and (b) spell out the 'preventive principles' or objectives that should inform the development and implementation of these arrangements.

xv Existing gaps in regulatory coverage should be addressed, notably by the development of new regulatory packages on such issues as the management of work transport, temporary working and sub-contracting, and the ergonomic design of work tasks and schedules. In addition, 'principles of prevention' should include the need for employers to adjust work to the physical and psychological capabilities of workers and, more generally, to protect and enhance the 'quality of working life'.

xvi A system of mobile union safety representatives should be established to cover smaller workplaces, and steps should be taken to equalise the representation rights provided to union and non-union workers. In addition, the powers of workplace representatives should be extended by the introduction of rights to 'stop the job' in prescribed circumstances of danger to health and safety, issue 'Provisional Improvement Notices' where it is believed there is a serious infringement of statutory health and safety standards, and enforce all of their rights through complaints to employment tribunals.

xvii There should be a substantial increase in Health and Safety Executive and local authority inspector numbers, together with the adoption of a more rigorous approach to the enforcement of health and safety laws, including a greater willingness to bring prosecutions and take cases on indictment to the Crown Court. These changes should be supported by raising the maximum levels of fines that can be imposed by magistrates, removing the current restrictions on the use of imprisonment, and the use of other penalties, such as 'proportionate fines' linked to company turnover or profits, 'equity' fines whereby fines would be paid in the form of new share capital, and 'corporate probation' orders. In addition the current manslaughter law should be changed to introduce a new offence of 'corporate killing' and facilitate the prosecution of directors who recklessly endanger worker health and safety, along with the imposition under the Health and Safety at Work Act 1974 of an explicit health and safety duty on directors.

xviii Workers who are injured at work should be entitled to full sick pay for a year, and attention should be paid to the adverse consequences for workers injured at work of the current trend away from final salary pension schemes.

xix A more generous and extensive system of no-fault compensation should be introduced to provide injured and ill workers with long-term benefits. In addition, in order to avoid the difficulties associated with establishing the work-related nature of many health conditions, consideration should be given to making such compensation available on a 'non-work-related' basis. The introduction of an expanded and more generous no-fault compensation system should be funded by employer contributions and these contributions should be 'performance-rated'. Consideration should also be given to operating this system on a sectoral and jointly controlled basis, in order to increase the potential for it to take on a more general preventive role via the provision of guidance and advice and, perhaps, the establishment of regional occupational health and safety services that can be utilised by smaller employers.

xx Employers should be required to appoint 'rehabilitation coordinators' and to develop rehabilitation plans for ill and injured workers whose absence from work exceeds, or is likely to exceed, a specified length of time.

# Chapter 5

# Equality and discrimination

5.1 Discrimination and inequality of opportunity are endemic in the UK, not least in the context of employment. Women earn less than men and experience both a glass ceiling and – of more importance to many – a sticky floor which traps them in low paid, frequently low quality work (particularly in the case of those who need to work part-time). Ethnic minority workers earn less than comparable white workers. The extent of the race-pay gap differs between various ethnic minority groups but workers of all such groups – other factors held constant – earn less than their white counterparts. While those with disabilities account for almost one fifth of the working age population, only one disabled person in 10 is in employment. Discrimination on grounds of sexual orientation, religion and belief and age flourish and those in significant decision-making positions in no sense reflect Britain's diverse population. The cost of discrimination and inequality is enormous and includes the social exclusion experienced by many young people – particularly those of African-Caribbean, Pakistani and Bangladeshi backgrounds – and by large numbers of the disabled, and huge levels of poverty among women who find themselves as lone parents or single in old age.

5.2 In total (on 2000 figures), the law relating to discrimination involves no fewer than 30 Acts of Parliament, 38 Statutory Instruments, 11 Codes of Practice and 12 European Community Directives and Recommendations. Discrimination law has developed piecemeal by way of response to immediate problems, and there is little consistency between the different statutory regimes. Each head of discrimination currently regulated by statute has its own responsible commission. These commissions are prohibited by law from sharing some types of information with each other. At present only discrimination on grounds of sex, race and disability are generally regulated. Over the next few years the UK is obliged by the EC Employment and Race Directives to introduce legislation regulating discrimination on grounds of sexual orientation, religion and belief and age, and must make significant amendments to race and disability legislation. It is likely that, within a similar time frame, amendments will be required to the regulation of sex discrimination, the EC Equal Treatment Directive being in the process of amendment to bring it into line with the EC Race Directive.

5.3 It is crucial that discrimination law undergoes a radical process of reform. All the indications are that the government does not plan any radical reform to implement European Community law, but intends rather to proceed with piecemeal additions and alterations to the already incoherent mass of discrimination law. The argument is being made that the time-scale involved requires the amendments to be made by way of regulations passed under the European Communities Act 1972. But this will only serve to make a bad situation worse. It is essential that the required additions and amendments be made as part of a completely restructured approach to discrimination law. What follows is an attempt to set out how such legislation might be framed and what its fundamental provisions ought to be. It should be noted that the current discrimination legislation applies not only to employment but also to access to goods and services, education and housing etc. A single Equality Act should similarly apply beyond the employment field. But given the remit of the Charter here proposed, we deal in this chapter only with the provisions which relate to employment (broadly defined).

### Recommendation

i    *The maze of confusing, complex and frequently contradictory discrimination legislation should be replaced with a single Equality Act.*

# Who should be protected from discrimination?

## Extending the protected grounds

5.4 At present the only grounds of discrimination against which relatively comprehensive protection against discrimination exists are race, sex, and disability. Legal protection against discrimination on grounds of married status and against direct discrimination connected with gender-reassignment is provided in the employment context. Those who are discriminated against in connection with their sexual orientation or religion are unprotected by law unless, in the latter

---

case, a sufficiently close connection exists between religion and race for discrimination on the grounds of the former to amount to discrimination – whether direct or indirect – on grounds of the latter. The EC Employment Directive, which must be implemented in stages from December 2003, will require the extension of protection against discrimination to age, religion and sexual orientation.

## Multiple discrimination

5.5 Particular problems arise for people who are vulnerable to discrimination on more than one ground. The comparative model adopted by current legislation requires that an applicant identify herself either as a woman, for example, or as black, Asian, etc, or as a person with a disability, a lesbian or a Muslim (the last two characterisations post-implementation of the EC Employment Directive). If she believes that she has been discriminated against as, for example, a Muslim woman in particular, she will have to rely separately on the Sex Discrimination Act and whatever provision is introduced to regulate discrimination on grounds of religion, if as a lesbian Asian woman on the Sex Discrimination Act, the Race Relations Act and whatever provision is introduced to regulate discrimination on grounds of sexual orientation. At the level of principle this approach to multiple discrimination is objectionable because it forces the applicant to disaggregate what is a single identity into component parts which are meaningful only in that discrimination based upon them is prohibited. It also in many cases involves the prioritisation of one or more characteristics over others – the applicant has to choose to identify herself primarily as black or female, Asian or lesbian, woman or Muslim.

5.6 The current approach also creates difficulties in practice because of the multiple comparisons required if more than one legislative provision is relied upon (the lesbian Asian woman will have to compare herself with a heterosexual Asian woman under the legislative provisions dealing with sexual orientation discrimination, with a lesbian non-Asian woman under the Race Relations Act and with a gay Asian man under the Sex Discrimination Act). In cases of direct discrimination she may be able to make out her case – if she was discriminated against precisely because she was a lesbian Asian women she ought to succeed under the sexual orientation provisions on the ground that a heterosexual Asian woman would not have been treated as she was, under the Race Relations Act on the ground that a lesbian non-Asian woman would not have been treated as she was, and under the Sex Discrimination Act on the ground that a gay Asian man would not have been treated as she was. But failure to

---

bring her claim under every possible legislative provision may result in her losing her case on the ground, for example (if she took it under the Sex Discrimination Act alone) that the reason for the discrimination was her sexual orientation or race rather than her sex.

5.7 It ought to be possible to avoid unnecessary complexity, duplication and the dismissal of meritorious claims by bringing **multiple discrimination** claims – here a claim to have been discriminated against as a lesbian Asian woman. To the extent that a tribunal found that the discrimination was on one or two, rather than all three related grounds, the decision could make this clear. Permitting multiple discrimination claims would have greater significance in the indirect discrimination context. Even if no statistical evidence as such is required to establish indirect discrimination, the concept entails at heart a comparison between the relative proportions of various groups which can comply with particular rules or practices. Where a practice impacts disproportionately on a person precisely because he is a Sikh man, for example, it may not be possible to demonstrate sufficient disparity in impact between Sikhs and non-Sikhs on the one hand, or between men and women on the other to challenge it as indirectly discriminatory on grounds of sex or race. (Equally, a practice which impacts disproportionately on Sudanese Muslim woman may not do so sufficiently on Muslims, Sudanese people or women in general to establish a relevant indirect discrimination claim.)

## 'Disability'

5.8 Many of the grounds suggested above ought to be included within those protected by legislation are self-explanatory. 'Disability' is not. The Disability Discrimination Act as it is currently drafted is significantly flawed in that it adopts a very narrow definition of disability and fails as a result to regulate many instances of discrimination in connection with a person's actual or perceived medical status (such as, for example, discrimination on the basis that a person is believed to have cancer, and discrimination on the grounds that a person is or is perceived to be HIV positive). The definition of direct discrimination proposed below would have the effect of extending protection from discrimination to those incorrectly regarded as suffering from a disability (ie. such discrimination would amount to discrimination 'on grounds of disability'). But it would not itself serve to protect those who are not functionally impaired (or not sufficiently functionally impaired to meet the current definition of disability) **but who are nonetheless discriminated against because of their health status.** The gap which exists in relation to HIV positive status applies also in relation to genetic conditions or predispositions to genetic conditions which do not themselves significantly impair people's everyday functioning but which may nevertheless render them vulnerable to discrimination.

5.9 The Northern Ireland Equality Commission proposes that the law be extended to cover perceived disability and those with a disability specific genetic disposition, and recommends that 'further work is undertaken to review the definition of disability', but stops short of calling as yet for a complete overhaul of the definition. We agree with the Commission that the generally asymmetrical nature of the prohibition on disability discrimination ought to remain undisturbed (that is, that as a general rule only those who are discriminated against because they are disabled, rather than because they are not) should be entitled to claim. But it is wholly unacceptable that people who are subject to discrimination on grounds of their medical status (real or perceived) are denied the protection of legislation. The current position is that the more irrational the discrimination (ie. the less a condition actually affects a person's day-to-day life), the more able an employer is to discriminate in connection with it. Nor is it clears that this position will be tenable once the disability-related provisions of the EC Employment Directive come into force.

### Recommendations

ii   *The proposed single Equality Act should regulate discrimination on grounds of sex, pregnancy, marital status[1], responsibility for dependents, sexual orientation, gender reassignment, religion or belief, age, disability, race, colour, nationality, ethnic or national origins.*

iii  *The proposed single Equality Act should make express provision for the regulation of discrimination on multiple grounds, and should adopt a wide definition of disability to extend the scope of the current legislation.*

# What does discrimination mean?

## Direct discrimination

5.10 Direct discrimination is generally accepted to mean less favourable treatment for on grounds of race, sex, disability, sexual orientation, etc. This is the formulation generally adopted in the

---

1   Defined, as in section 2 of Ireland's Employment Equality Act 1998, as 'being single, married, separated, divorced or widowed'.

---

existing and proposed legislation, save that the Sex Discrimination Act currently prohibits only less favourable treatment on the grounds of the claimant's sex. The significance of the wider formulation is that it extends, for example, to less favourable treatment on grounds that a worker refused to discriminate against someone else (*Weathersfield Limited v Sargent*). There is no principled reason for the distinction between the Sex Discrimination Act and the other legislation (existing and proposed in relation to the implementation of the Employment Directive), and the broader formulation should be used across the board. In our view the prohibition on discrimination on grounds of sex should thus extend to discrimination against a person because of someone else's sex.

5.11 The Disability Discrimination Act currently adopts a different approach to discrimination, prohibiting (a) less favourable treatment for a reason which relates to the disabled person's disability, and (b) a failure to make a reasonable adjustment. Both forms of discrimination are capable of justification in line with a currently low threshold. Less favourable treatment for a reason which relates to the disabled person's disability looks on its face to be the same as direct discrimination under the current Sex Discrimination Act formulation but it is wider: in *Clark v TDG Ltd (t/a Novacold)* the Court of Appeal confirmed that this type of discrimination would extend to less favourable treatment by reason of a disabled person's absence from work, where the absence was connected with the person's disability. This would not qualify as direct discrimination under the Sex Discrimination Act or Race Relations Act, save in the exceptional case in which the reason for less favourable treatment is a woman's pregnancy or maternity-related absence (*Webb v EMO (No.2)*), this as a result of the decision of the European Court of Justice in the same case).

5.12 The wider formulation adopted by the Disability Discrimination Act appears attractive, but it must be borne in mind that, at present, all disability discrimination is capable of justification. The government proposes to implement the EC Employment Directive by withdrawing the general justification defence in relation to disability discrimination which is 'direct' as that concept is defined by the Race Relations Act and Sex Discrimination Act. It is perhaps inevitable that any broader definition of discrimination will (and indeed ought to) be coupled with a general justification defence (as distinct from the narrow and specific 'genuine occupational qualification' defences to direct discrimination permitted by the Sex Discrimination Act and Race Relations Act). For this reason, and to avoid having to import a general justification defence in relation to discrimination (direct as well as indirect) it is better to stick with a relatively narrow definition of 'direct discrimination'. This is particularly the case given that the proposed extension of protected grounds will include grounds such as age and having dependents (as well as disability) discrimination. The definition of direct discrimination should be extended expressly to include harassment.

## Indirect discrimination

5.13 The most significant problem associated with the meaning of indirect discrimination is the proliferation of definitions which apply between:

(a) the employment-related provisions of the Sex Discrimination Act as amended by the Burden of Proof Regulations;

(b) the non-employment related provisions of the Sex Discrimination Act;

(c) the Race Relations Act as it is likely to be amended to comply with the Race Directive;

(d) the test applied by the European Court of Justice in the context of nationality discrimination (*O'Flynn v Adjudication Officer*);

(e) the test adopted by the EC Employment Directive and applicable to sexual orientation, age and religion and belief; and

(f) the test which applies in relation to disability.

5.14 Space forbids detailed discussion of the various tests. That which appears to be the most generous to the applicant, and which is best placed to cover multiple discrimination, is that adopted by the European Court of Justice in *O'Flynn* which formed the starting point for European Community discussions on the Race and Employment Directives. It provides that indirect discrimination shall be taken to occur where conditions (practices, policies, etc.) are imposed which are *intrinsically liable* to affect persons of a protected group more than others and, by doing so, to place them at a particular disadvantage (this subject to a justification defence). (A 'protected group' is a group of persons defined by reference to a 'protected ground' – ie. a group defined by sex, nationality, sexual orientation, disability, having dependents, being pregnant, etc.)

5.15 The test for justification proposed below echoes the approach taken in the context of sex discrimination by the European Court of Justice, and in the context of indirect discrimination it may not be possible to formulate any tighter or more specific provision. It should be noted that this formulation is significantly tighter than that which applies, by virtue of the Disability Discrimination Act, to both **direct** and **indirect** disability-related discrimination (*Jones v*

*Post Office*). The difficulties associated with proving indirect discrimination on multiple grounds were pointed out above. It may be impossible for a Sikh man to demonstrate sufficient disparity of impact between Sikhs and non-Sikhs on the one hand, or between men and women on the other, to challenge a practice which disadvantages him as indirectly discriminatory on grounds of sex or race (or, from July 2002 religion). But as a Sikh man he ought nevertheless to be in a position to challenge that practice if it disproportionately disadvantages him because of his simultaneous membership of these two 'protected groups'.

## Disability discrimination

5.16 A further issue which needs to be addressed concerns disability discrimination. At present the Disability Discrimination Act does not prohibit indirect disability discrimination as such, although its definition of 'discrimination' encompasses much that would otherwise be regarded as indirect discrimination, while the duty of reasonable accommodation performs a similar function albeit in a different form. Having said this, the duty to adjust applies only in relation to:

(a) arrangements made by or on behalf of the employer 'for determining to whom employment should be offered';

(b) 'any term, condition or arrangements on which employment, promotion, a transfer, training or any other benefit is offered or afforded'; or

(c) 'any physical feature of premises occupied by an employer'.

It does not apply, in particular, to dismissal (though it will apply to steps taken prior to dismissal), and it does not apply in respect of matters which are not 'job-related' (*Kenny v Hampshire Constabulary*). The domestic approach to disability discrimination will have to be modified to comply with the EC Employment Directive which requires that indirect disability discrimination be prohibited (subject to justification, discussed below) or that the duty to make reasonable adjustments applies to all situations in which a worker could otherwise complain of indirect discrimination.

## Recommendations

*iv*    *The proposed single Equality Act should define direct discrimination as occurring where one person is treated less favourably than another is, has been or would be treated in a comparable situation, on one or more of the protected grounds (ie. sex, race, disability, etc). It should provide, 'for the avoidance of doubt', that less favourable treatment will be 'on the protected grounds':*

(a)   where the reason is specific to those grounds;

(b)   where those grounds apply to a person other than the person subjected to the less favourable treatment (ie. when a person is less favourably treated because of another person's sex, race, etc); and

(c)   where the less favourable treatment to which a person is subjected is on the grounds that he or she is perceived to have a protected characteristic (characteristic of sex, race, disability, etc).

The Equality Act should provide that, when an applicant complains of direct discrimination on more than one of the protected grounds, a tribunal may find the complaint well founded on each or any of the grounds if it is satisfied that that ground was a cause (though not the only or principal cause) of the less favourable treatment complained of. The Act should also expressly apply to harassment, defined to mean unwanted conduct related to any of the protected grounds which takes place with the purpose or effect of violating the dignity of a person or of creating an intimidating, hostile, degrading, humiliating or offensive environment.

v     The proposed single Equality Act should define indirect discrimination as occurring where an apparently neutral provision, criterion or practice is intrinsically liable to put persons of a protected group at a particular disadvantage compared to other persons, unless that provision, criterion or practice is objectively justified by a legitimate aim and the means of achieving that aim are appropriate and necessary.

vi    The proposed single Equality Act should define indirect discrimination as occurring where an apparently neutral provision, criterion or practice is intrinsically liable to put persons of a group defined by reference to more than one protected ground at a particular disadvantage compared with other persons, unless that provision, criterion or practice is objectively justified by a legitimate aim and the means of achieving that aim are appropriate and necessary.

vii   The proposed single Equality Act should provide that the duty to make reasonable adjustments to the needs of disabled workers will apply in all circumstances in which indirect discrimination might be established.

# Are there circumstances in which discrimination should be permissible?

## Genuine occupational requirements

5.17   A unified and coherent approach to discrimination law does not entail treating all grounds of discrimination in the same way. There will be many cases in which direct age discrimination is appropriate (these will include, but are not limited to, restrictions on the employment of young persons). By contrast, there are very few situations in which direct race discrimination would be regarded as acceptable. The appropriate way of dealing with the question of when and if direct discrimination on any of the protected grounds may be justified is, for the most part, by establishing a genuine occupational requirement defence. This concept has operated satisfactorily since the implementation of the Race Relations Act and Sex Discrimination Act, and will have to be substituted for the current approach taken by the Disability Discrimination Act with the implementation of the Employment Directive. In addition, specific and express additional exceptions to the prohibition of direct discrimination may be required in relation to age and disability discrimination (considered below). Contrary to the position permitted by the Employment Directive, there should be no provision permitting discrimination against same-sex couples in relation to their married counterparts.

5.18 The change in terminology from the current formulation ('genuine occupational *qualifications*') proposed below is intended to narrow the provisions and is in any case required to render domestic legislation compatible with the Race and Employment Directives. This formulation is taken directly from the text of the Employment and Race Directives. Its omission of the special provision made by the former to deal with discrimination by religious bodies is deliberate. To the extent that such discrimination is within the genuine occupational requirement defence it should be regarded as justified (this might include, for example, the position of a carer in a religious care home and, to the extent that such staff were actually engaged in pastoral duties, that of a cleaner also, as well as the more obvious position of director or chaplain of such an institution). But it has the benefit of tightening the current formulation (see Article 4(2) of the Directive and its proposed transposition into domestic law) and clarifying, for example, that discrimination on grounds of sexual orientation may be justified only where the characteristic of (for example, not being gay) constitutes a genuine, *legitimate* and *proportionate* determining occupational requirement.

## Positive discrimination and permissible age discrimination

5.19 The genuine occupational requirement defence set out above applies only when the discrimination at issue is connected with the requirements of the particular job. But among the other circumstances in which discrimination in the employment field ought perhaps to be acceptable are in cases of *positive discrimination.* Whereas being an Asian woman might properly be regarded as a genuine occupational requirement for a counselling job in a centre for victims of domestic violence whose clients are predominantly Asian, or being a gay man a genuine occupational requirement for some types of HIV/AIDs related work, the defence would not apply in a situation in which an employer wished to give preference to particular categories of worker who were under-represented either in the employer's own workforce or in the workforce more generally. Yet such positive discrimination, much of which is currently prohibited by domestic legislation, may be necessary in order to counteract the effects of past and present discrimination. Many other jurisdictions permit (and, on occasion, require) positive discrimination. Further, such discrimination has come to be accepted within the European Community legislative framework.

5.20 A different question is whether there are other circumstances in which discrimination in the employment field may be acceptable. One of the most significant questions which arises here concerns *age discrimination.* The EC Employment Directive provides that:

'...Member States may provide that differences of treatment on grounds of age shall not constitute discrimination, if, within the context of national law, they are objectively and reasonably justified by a legitimate aim, including legitimate employment policy, labour market and vocational training objectives, and if the means of achieving that aim are appropriate and necessary.'

The comprehensive prohibition of age discrimination in employment would entail the abolition of retirement ages and special protective provisions dealing with young workers, neither being adequately covered by the genuine occupational requirement defence. The latter is clearly inadvisable while the former creates significant problems, not least because of the effect on young people seeking to enter the job market and the possibility that those who ought to be enjoying retirement will be coerced into continuing work. No-one would expect a law enabling an airline pilots or air traffic controllers to continue to work indefinitely. Firefighters and the police are also expected to retire from front-line service at 55. Others in potentially highly stressed and safety-critical roles can perhaps expect to be obliged to retire – on good pensions – at a similar age. There is also the problem of upper-end jobs, not least because of the historical restriction of access to those jobs predominantly to otherwise privileged white men. It was reported in May 2002 that proposals will be put in the autumn to a summit of European Ministers and the

United Nations in Berlin to scrap retirement ages across the Continent. While removing retirement ages would not itself require any changes to pensionable ages, the economic pressure towards increases in pensionable ages cannot be ignored. It is vital that a focus on the eradication of age discrimination is not used to obscure an attack on current pension entitlement.

## Recommendations

viii *The proposed single Equality Act should provide that a difference of treatment which is based on a characteristic related to any of the protected grounds shall not constitute discrimination where, by reason of the nature of the particular occupational activities concerned or of the context in which they are carried out, such a characteristic constitutes a genuine and determining occupational requirement, provided that the objective is legitimate and the requirement is proportionate.*

ix *The proposed single Equality Act should provide that it shall be lawful for an employer, with a view to ensuring full equality in practice, to adopt or maintain specific measures to prevent or compensate for disadvantages linked to any of the protected grounds, provided that any discrimination is proportionate to the aim pursued.*

x *The proposed single Equality Act should permit certain types of age discrimination. The justification for such discrimination would lie in labour market policy rather than the needs of the job itself or (as is necessary for the justification of indirect discrimination) of the employer.*

# What discriminatory conduct by employers should be unlawful?

## The scope of protection

5.21 The coverage of the existing discrimination provisions, while wide, is not comprehensive. Problems have arisen, in particular, in relation to workers not under an obligation personally to perform the work or services at issue (as in *Mirror Group Newspapers v Gunning*, in which the alleged discrimination was against a very small family business). Equally problematic has been the position of volunteers, office holders and ex-employees who have been denied the protection of the Acts. It is imperative that all be protected from unjustified discrimination on the protected grounds. At present there are a number of indefensible distinctions between the statutory regimes as a result of (for example) European Court of Justice decisions which impact only in relation to sex discrimination and have even in that context been very narrowly read by the domestic courts; and the recent Race and Employment Directives which do not apply to sex discrimination. The position needs to be harmonised.

## Discrimination and the Equal Pay Act 1970

5.22 The Sex Discrimination Act does not, at present, apply to discrimination in contractual terms, the Equal Pay Act instead permitting challenges to pay discrimination between (solely) those workers who are employed in jobs which are similar, which have been rated as equally valuable by the employer or which a tribunal determines are of equal value. The Equal Pay Act is unnecessarily complex and cumbersome and serves to protect from challenge much pay-related discrimination. Passed in order to assist the eradication of sex discrimination in pay, it has in fact proven incredibly difficult to use successfully. If it were replaced, cases of sex-related pay discrimination could be challenged under the single Equality Act and there would be no restriction on the comparators (real or hypothetical) by which women could establish pay discrimination. Coupled with the proactive obligations on employers proposed below this will be a much more effective statutory regime.

### Recommendations

xi    *The proposed single Equality Act should apply its protection from discrimination as widely as possible, that is: to volunteers and office holders as well as 'employees'; to legal persons as well as individuals; and to ex-employees as well as to prospective and current workers.*

xii    *The proposed single Equality Act should adopt the following formulation to the prohibition of discrimination in the employment context:*

*It is unlawful for a person, in relation to employment by that person at an establishment in Great Britain, to discriminate against another*

*(a)  in the arrangements the employer makes for the purpose of determining who should be offered that employment; or*

*(b)  in the terms on which that employment is offered; or*

*(c)  by refusing or deliberately omitting to offer the other that employment.*

*It is unlawful for a person, in the case of a person employed by that person at an establishment in Great Britain, to discriminate against the worker –*

*(a)  in the terms of employment afforded to the worker or*

*(b)  in the way that worker is afforded access to opportunities for promotion, transfer or training, or to any other benefits, facilities or services, or by refusing or deliberately omitting to afford him or her access to them; or*

(c)  *by dismissing that worker, or subjecting the worker to any other detriment.*

*It is unlawful for an employer to discriminate against a person who was formerly a worker in relation to any matter connected with that employment in the provision of benefits or by subjecting that worker to any other detriment.*

xiii  *Sex discrimination in relation to pay and other contractual terms should be regulated by the proposed single Equality Act rather than the Equal Pay Act. As is recommended below, however, this 'individual' model for challenge to pay and other forms of discrimination must be complemented by positive duties on employers.*

# Enforcement

## Auditing and monitoring by employees

5.23 Employment-related (and other) discrimination remains endemic even in relation to those grounds which have been the subject of more or less comprehensive legislation for more than a quarter of a century. One of the most significant reasons for this is the individualistic enforcement mechanisms which apply. It is essential that the individual enforcement routes be supplemented by the imposition of duties upon employers to take active steps to scrutinise their employment practices for evidence of discrimination and to eliminate any such discrimination. Legislation along these lines has been in place in Ontario, Canada (though only in relation to sex-related pay discrimination) for some years and many valuable lessons have been learned from this experience. What monitoring obligations can do is to render transparent the relationship within organisations between sex, race etc, on the one hand; and workplace position and pay on the other. Once this is done, employers ought to be required to work with recognised trade unions in seeking to determine the extent to which occupational position and pay result from discrimination (direct and indirect) and in taking action to eliminate such discrimination.

## Addressing the impact of workplace segregation on pay

5.24 Collective action of the type set out above depends on there being a sufficient body of relatively advantaged workers (male, white, etc.) in order to provide comparators for the purpose of establishing less favourable treatment. Comparisons ought to be undertaken not only between 'comparable jobs' but also between jobs of different value to determine whether those predominantly done by women are being rewarded proportionately to those (more or less 'valuable') predominantly done by men. But while such employer action can help to remedy the discrimination which occurs within workplaces, it will not affect pay differences which arise between workplaces and by virtue of industrial and workplace sex and race segregation. The segregation itself may be reduced in the long term by more effective enforcement (not least the imposition of obligations on employers to monitor recruitment and to take steps to eliminate discrimination uncovered by such monitoring). But while it remains it has significant implications for the sex and race-related pay gaps. In addition to the imposition of positive duties on employers a serious commitment to the eradication of unjustified discrimination would make use of levers such as the award of public contracts to employers who make genuine efforts to address workplace discrimination.

## Improving individual enforcement and remedies

5.25 The individual approach to pay discrimination has been a failure in the United Kingdom. Some women have benefited from the Equal Pay Act. But many more have not. And despite the pay differentials suffered by ethnic minority workers pay-related race discrimination claims are almost unheard of. The other enforcement issue which must thus be addressed concerns the inadequacy of the individual enforcement mechanism as an individual enforcement mechanism. While compensation for discrimination is unlimited (except in the case of unintentional indirect race discrimination, the lack of compensation available for which must be addressed), tribunals may make recommendations only in relation to the individual applicants and are not, according to the decision of the Employment Appeal Tribunal in *North West Thames Regional Health Authority v Noone*, empowered to recommend that an applicant discriminated against in recruitment be offered the next job vacancy which arises. Tribunals should be given greater powers in this regard, and be armed with a more flexible range of remedies.

### Recommendations

xiv  *Obligations ought to be imposed on employers to monitor their employment practices for discriminatory impact and to eliminate such discrimination. Where no recognised union is present, scrutiny and remedial action ought to be required to be undertaken in conjunction with employee representatives.*

xv  *The under-payment of women and ethnic minority workers who are clustered in low-paying workplaces should be addressed by a mechanism whereby equality adjustments gained in workplaces in*

---

*which trade unions are recognised and have been involved in the elimination of pay discrimination are extended to other workplaces. Consideration would have to be given to the basis on which workplaces could be regarded as sufficiently similar to permit this extension. The Central Arbitration Committee would be the most suitable body to perform this task.*

xvi *Measures such as contract compliance must be utilised in order to tackle discrimination in pay, working conditions and access to jobs and promotion and the equality commissions (or single Equality Commission) must be given strengthened powers of formal investigation more effectively to tackle endemic discrimination in various sectors of the labour market or by individual employers.*

xvii *Tribunals ought to be given the power to order discriminators to alter their practices and, in suitable recruitment cases, to offer the successful applicant the next available job.*

xviii *In cases in which a successful applicant is representative of a number of others (whether as a woman in an undervalued female job or otherwise) tribunals ought to be able to provide remedies which apply not only to the applicant but to others in similar relevant circumstances.*

# Conclusion

i    The maze of confusing, complex and frequently contradictory discrimination legislation should be replaced with a single Equality Act.

## Who should be protected from discrimination?

ii   The proposed single Equality Act should regulate discrimination on grounds of sex, pregnancy, marital status[2], responsibility for dependents, sexual orientation, gender reassignment, religion or belief, age, disability, race, colour, nationality, ethnic or national origins.

iii  The proposed single Equality Act should make express provision for the regulation of discrimination on multiple grounds, and should adopt a wide definition of disability to extend the scope of the current legislation.

## What does discrimination mean?

iv   The proposed single Equality Act should define direct discrimination as occurring where one person is treated less favourably than another is, has been or would be treated in a comparable situation, on one or more of the protected grounds (ie. sex, race, disability, etc.). It should provide, 'for the avoidance of doubt', that less favourable treatment will be 'on the protected grounds':

(a) where the reason is *specific* to those grounds;

(b) where those grounds apply to a person other than the person subjected to the less favourable treatment (ie. when a person is less favourably treated because of *another* person's sex, race, etc); and

(c) where the less favourable treatment to which a person is subjected is on the grounds that he or she is *perceived* to have a protected characteristic (characteristic of sex, race, disability, etc).

The Equality Act should provide that, when an applicant complains of direct discrimination on more than one of the protected grounds, a tribunal may find

---

2  Defined, as in section 2 of Ireland's Employment Equality Act 1998, as 'being single, married, separated, divorced or widowed'.

the complaint well founded on each or any of the grounds if it is satisfied that that ground was a cause (though not the only or principal cause) of the less favourable treatment complained of. The Act should also expressly apply to harassment, defined to mean unwanted conduct related to any of the protected grounds which takes place with the purpose or effect of violating the dignity of a person or of creating an intimidating, hostile, degrading, humiliating or offensive environment.

v    The proposed single Equality Act should define indirect discrimination as occurring where an apparently neutral provision, criterion, or practice is intrinsically liable to put persons of a protected group at a particular disadvantage compared to other persons, unless that provision, criterion or practice is objectively justified by a legitimate aim and the means of achieving that aim are appropriate and necessary.

vi   The proposed single Equality Act should also define indirect discrimination as occurring where an apparently neutral provision, criterion or practice is intrinsically liable to put persons of a group defined by reference to more than one protected ground at a particular disadvantage compared with other persons, unless that provision, criterion or practice is objectively justified by a legitimate aim and the means of achieving that aim are appropriate and necessary.

vii  The proposed single Equality Act should provide that the duty to make reasonable adjustments to the needs of disabled workers will apply in all circumstances in which indirect discrimination might be established.

## Are there circumstances in which discrimination should be permissable?

viii The proposed single Equality Act should provide that a difference of treatment which is based on a characteristic related to any of the protected grounds shall not constitute discrimination where, by reason of the nature of the particular occupational activities concerned or of the context in which they are carried out, such a characteristic constitutes a genuine and determining occupational *requirement*, provided that the objective is legitimate and the requirement is proportionate.

ix  The proposed single Equality Act should provide that it shall be lawful for an employer, with a view to ensuring full equality in practice, to adopt or maintain specific measures to prevent or compensate for disadvantages linked to any of the protected grounds, provided that any discrimination is proportionate to the aim pursued.

x  The proposed single Equality Act should permit certain types of age discrimination. The justification for such discrimination would lie in labour market policy rather than the needs of the job itself or (as is necessary for the justification of indirect discrimination) of the employer.

## What discriminatory conduct by employers should be unlawful?

xi  The proposed single Equality Act should apply its protection from discrimination as widely as possible, that is: to volunteers and office holders as well as 'employees'; to legal persons as well as individuals; and to ex-employees as well as to prospective and current workers.

xii  The proposed single Equality Act should adopt the following formulation to the prohibition of discrimination in the employment context:
It is unlawful for a person, in relation to employment by that person at an establishment in Great Britain, to discriminate against another
(a)  in the arrangements the employer makes for the purpose of determining who should be offered that employment; or
(b)  in the terms on which that employment is offered; or
(c)  by refusing or deliberately omitting to offer the other that employment.
It is unlawful for a person, in the case of a person employed by that person at an establishment in Great Britain, to discriminate against the worker –
(a)  in the terms of employment afforded to the worker or

(b)  in the way that worker is afforded access to opportunities for promotion, transfer or training, or to any other benefits, facilities or services, or by refusing or deliberately omitting to afford him or her access to them; or

(c)  by dismissing that worker, or subjecting the worker to any other detriment.

It is unlawful for an employer to discriminate against a person who was formerly a worker in relation to any matter connected with that employment in the provision of benefits or by subjecting that worker to any other detriment.

xiii Sex discrimination in relation to pay and other contractual terms should be regulated instead by the proposed single Equality Act rather than the Equal Pay Act. As is recommended below, however, this 'individual' model for challenge to pay and other forms of discrimination must be complemented by positive duties on employers.

## Enforcement

xiv Obligations ought to be imposed on employers to monitor their employment practices for discriminatory impact and to eliminate such discrimination. Where no recognised union is present, scrutiny and remedial action ought to be required to be undertaken in conjunction with employee representatives.

xv The under-payment of women and ethnic minority workers who are clustered in low-paying workplaces should be addressed by a mechanism whereby equality adjustments gained in workplaces in which trade unions are recognised and have been involved in the elimination of pay discrimination are extended to other workplaces. Consideration would have to be given to the basis on which workplaces could be regarded as sufficiently similar to permit this extension. The Central Arbitration Committee would be the most suitable body to perform this task.

xvi Measures such as contract compliance must be utilised in order to tackle discrimination in pay, working conditions and access to jobs and promotion

and the equality commissions (or single Equality
Commission) must be given strengthened powers of
formal investigation more effectively to tackle
endemic discrimination in various sectors of the
labour market or by individual employers.

xvii Tribunals ought to be given the power to order
discriminators to alter their practices and, in suitable
recruitment cases, to offer the successful applicant the
next available job.

xviii In cases in which a successful applicant is
representative of a number of others (whether as a
woman in an undervalued female job or otherwise)
tribunals ought to be able to provide remedies which
apply not only to the applicant but to others in similar
relevant circumstances.

A Charter of Workers' Rights

# Chapter 6

# Trade union freedom

6.1 The rights of trade unions and trade unionists are well established in international law. Trade union rights are just as much fundamental human rights as are the other human rights identified by international law such as the right to privacy, freedom of religion, and freedom of expression. At the heart of trade union rights is the fundamental freedom of workers to act together for mutual support through trade unions without State or employer interference. The rationale for this freedom is not that trade unions should enjoy special privileges but that, across the globe, trade unions are the prime means by which the imbalance in power between workers and employers can be redressed. Trade unions and trade unionists must therefore be protected from employer and State limitations on the freedom to act collectively.

6.2 It must be said at the outset that trade union rights (like other civil, political and social rights) are not unlimited: they do not give complete freedom to unions to do what they want. In a civilised society everyone and every organisation must accept limits on their freedom in order to respect the freedoms of others. Happily, where the line is to be drawn around trade union rights is clear from the very large body of international law on the subject. That is not to say that there is not scope for argument at the very fringes of trade union rights about what is or should be protected by international law, but as far as the UK is concerned, for the most part its trade union laws fall very clearly on one side of the line or the other so that there is very little room for debate.

6.3 Conventions 87 and 98 of the ILO and articles 5 and 6 of the Council of Europe's Social Charter make a convenient base from which fundamental trade union rights can be identified. The UK has ratified these provisions though, unlike the European Convention on

Human Rights and Fundamental Freedoms (made part of UK law by the Human Rights Act 1998), these provisions have not been made part of national law. This means that notwithstanding that the UK is bound by these international laws, UK citizens cannot enforce them directly in the UK courts (though since the *Wilson and Palmer* decision of the European Court of Human Rights they and the decisions of their supervisory bodies will have to be given increased respect).

---

## Convention No.87 on Freedom of Association and Protection of the Right to Organise, 1948

*Article 1*

Each Member of the International Labour Organisation for which this Convention is in force undertakes to give effect to the following provisions.

*Article 2*

Workers and employers, without distinction whatsoever, shall have the right to establish and, subject only to the rules of the organisation concerned, to join organisations of their own choosing without previous authorisation.

*Article 3*

1. Workers' and employers' organisations shall have the right to draw up their constitutions and rules, to elect their representatives in full freedom, to organise their administration and activities and to formulate their programmes.

2. The public authorities shall refrain from any interference which would restrict this right or impede the lawful exercise thereof.

*Article 4*

Workers' and employers' organisations shall not be liable to be dissolved or suspended by administrative authority.

*Article 5*

Workers' and employers' organisations shall have the right to establish and join federations and confederations and any such organisation, federation or confederation shall have the right to affiliate with international organisations of workers and employers.

*Article 6*

The provisions of Articles 2, 3 and 4 hereof apply to federations and confederations of workers' and employers' organisations.

*Article 7*

The acquisition of legal personality by workers' and employers' organisations, federations and confederations shall not be made subject to conditions of such a character as to restrict the application of the provisions of Articles 2, 3 and 4 hereof.

---

*Article 8*

1. In exercising the rights provided for in this Convention workers and employers and their respective organisations, like other persons or organised collectivities, shall respect the law of the land.

2. The law of the land shall not be such as to impair, nor shall it be so applied as to impair, the guarantees provided for in this Convention.

...

*Article 11*

Each Member of the International Labour Organisation for which this Convention is in force undertakes to take all necessary and appropriate measures to ensure that workers and employers may exercise freely the right to organise.

...

# Convention No.98 on the Right to Organise and to Bargain Collectively, 1949

*Article 1*

1. Workers shall enjoy adequate protection against acts of anti-union discrimination in respect of their employment.

2. Such protection shall apply more particularly in respect of acts calculated to –

(a) make the employment of a worker subject to the condition that he shall not join a union or shall relinquish trade union membership;

(b) cause the dismissal of or otherwise prejudice a worker by reason of union membership or because of participation in union activities outside working hours or, with the consent of the employer, within working hours.

*Article 2*

1. Workers' and employers' organisations shall enjoy adequate protection against any acts of interference by each other or each other's agents or members in their establishment, functioning or administration.

2. In particular, acts which are designed to promote the establishment of workers' organisations under the domination of employers or employers' organisations, or to support workers' organisations by financial or other means, with the object of placing such organisations under the control of employers or employers' organisations, shall be deemed to constitute acts of interference within the meaning of this Article.

*Article 3*

Machinery appropriate to national conditions shall be established, where necessary, for the purpose of ensuring respect for the right to organise as defined in the preceding Articles.

*Article 4*

Measures appropriate to national conditions shall be taken, where

necessary, to encourage and promote the full development and utilisation of machinery for voluntary negotiation between employers or employers' organisations and workers' organisations, with a view to the regulation of terms and conditions of employment by means of collective agreements.
...

## European Social Charter 1961

*Article 5 – The right to organise*

With a view to ensuring or promoting the freedom of workers and employers to form local, national or international organisations for the protection of their economic and social interests and to join those organisations, the Contracting Parties undertake that national law shall not be such as to impair, nor shall it be so applied as to impair, this freedom. The extent to which the guarantees provided for in this article shall apply to the police shall be determined by national laws or regulations. The principle governing the application to the members of the armed forces of these guarantees and the extent to which they shall apply to persons in this category shall equally be determined by national laws or regulations.

*Article 6 – The right to bargain collectively*

With a view to ensuring the effective exercise of the right to bargain collectively, the Contracting Parties undertake:

1. to promote joint consultation between workers and employers;

2. to promote, where necessary and appropriate, machinery for voluntary negotiations between employers or employers' organisations and workers' organisations, with a view to the regulation of terms and conditions of employment by means of collective agreements;

3. to promote the establishment and use of appropriate machinery for conciliation and voluntary arbitration for the settlement of labour disputes; and recognise:

4. the right of workers and employers to collective action in cases of conflicts of interest, including the right to strike, subject to obligations that might arise out of collective agreements previously entered into.

6.4 Various terms can be used to describe the rights to be found in these instruments (as lawyers call them): the right to organise, to trade union autonomy, of representation, to bargain collectively. They are all aspects of freedom of association: the rights to form and to join a trade union. This fundamental right is set out in every human rights document mentioned in chapter 1. For the purposes of this chapter it is convenient to classify the trade union rights derived from international law as follows:

- The right of unions to determine their own rule-book and constitution free from State and employer interference;

- The right of unions to have a legal status that enables them to defend themselves and carry out their functions effectively;
- The right of unions to raise funds and to spend them as they see fit;
- The right of unions to determine their own activities (including industrial action);
- The right of unions to bargain collectively and to represent their members;
- The right of members to be collectively bargained for and to be represented;
- The right of members to be protected from discrimination by the State or by employers; a protection that extends to discrimination on grounds of union membership or participation in union activities or for being represented or seeking to be represented by a union; and including protection for taking industrial action (including not crossing a picket line).

6.5 The right to representation, collective bargaining and against anti-union discrimination (other than for taking industrial action) are dealt with in chapter 7. This chapter deals with the other fundamental rights listed above. These can all be put under the heading of the right to trade union autonomy, a phrase which means the right of trade unions to decide for themselves their rules and methods of self-government, their activities and how they raise and spend their funds. It is not for the State, employers, or judicial perceptions of "the public interest" to dictate these matters. Nevertheless, the right to trade union self-determination is not absolute and trade unions must comply with the general laws against discrimination and so on. But international law has developed clear boundaries within which trade unions must be given full autonomy.

6.6 In this chapter UK law is measured against the right of trade union autonomy and the limitations on it permitted by international law. Recommendations are made for the changes to UK law necessary to make it consistent with the UK's international legal obligations. Notwithstanding government assertions to the contrary, the UK is in breach of international laws it has ratified in respect of most of these points. Indeed the Prime Minister's often quoted statement of 31 March 1997 remains an entirely accurate description of the current state of the law under Labour's second term (save that the proposals to which he refers have become law):

> It was claimed... that employers will not be able to dismiss people on strike. Untrue. That employees will get full employment rights from their first day. Wrong.
>
> Let me state the position clearly, so that no one is in any doubt. The

*essential elements of the trade union legislation of the 1980s will remain. There will be no return to secondary action, flying pickets, strikes without ballots, the closed shop and all the rest.*

*The changes that we do propose would leave British law the most restrictive on trade unions in the western world.*

In the face of annual condemnation by the international law supervisory bodies (see below) of that state of affairs in the UK, it is not easy to understand junior ministers who appear to dispute Mr Blair's analysis to assert that the government conforms to its international obligations.

---

## Britain and the ILO

The government strongly condemn international violation of the rights of trade unions, their members, and their members' families. We fully support the work of the International Labour Organisation, which is the UN specialist agency with specific responsibility for protecting and promoting workers' rights worldwide.

The ILO was founded in 1919, at an important point in our history. It is no coincidence that that happened at the end of the first world war, and the ILO's goal was to promote peace through social justice, and to recognise internationally human rights and labour rights. Its tripartite structure, which enables workers' and employers' organisations to participate equally with governments, is unique in the UN system.

In 1948 – shortly after another world war, and again I think that that is no coincidence – a convention on freedom of association and protection of the right to organise was launched. The UK was the first country to ratify the convention, and we are proud of that. The right to organise is fundamental to democracy, yet my hon. Friend reminded us that even in the 21st century trade union rights are being violated around the world.
...

Some 140 countries have now ratified the ILO convention on freedom of association and protection of the right to organise. In 1998, more than 50 years after adopting that convention, all 175 member states of the ILO signed up to a declaration of rights and fundamental principles at work. All those member states agreed to respect, promote and realise the ILO core labour standards, regardless of their level of economic development and – crucially – whether or not they had ratified the relevant ILO conventions.

The ILO's core labour standards cover freedom of association, promotion of collective bargaining, abolition of forced and child labour and the elimination of discrimination in employment. The United Kingdom played a leading role in securing the 1998 declaration, and we continue to support the follow-up process to the declaration.

The government provide substantial financial support to the ILO.

---

Chapter 6 : Trade union freedom

Equally importantly, we also work closely with the organisation to ensure that the international framework to combat abuses of workers' rights throughout the world is in place and effective.

...The UK has continually supported the ILO's work in defending trade union rights. We have ratified all the ILO core conventions, including those relating to freedom of association and collective bargaining, and we encourage other countries to do so.

...We should not forget that one of the first acts of the Labour government was to honour the pledge to restore trade union rights at government communications headquarters, Cheltenham – a more recent episode in our history. That was in conformity with our ILO obligations, following ILO criticism of previous UK government policy.

...I want to assure the House that the government will continue to work actively and constructively with our partners in all international forums to promote the implementation of all ILO core labour standards and to bring an end to the violations and abuses of the rights of our fellow human beings.

*Malcolm Wicks (Parliamentary Under-Secretary of State for Work and Pensions)*, HC Debs, 27 June 2002, col.1069

# The right of unions to determine their own rulebook and constitution free from State and employer interference

6.7 It is essential that unions as democratic bodies are entitled to draw up their own rulebooks setting out their constitutions. Of course, if a union breaches its own rulebook it can be sued by an affected member. The autonomy required here is to protect unions from outside interference from the State or employers. In the UK, the State, through law, does encroach on trade union constitutions to a significant degree, and for this and other reasons British law has been criticised by the supervisory bodies of the ILO and the European Social Charter.

## Union elections

6.8 One particular aspect which is inconsistent with trade union autonomy is that the law and not the unions or their members dictate that union presidents, general secretaries and executive committee members are elected by postal ballot every five years. But the ILO has concluded that this incursion into trade union autonomy is not inconsistent with the Conventions and it is so well accepted amongst the unions today that there is little call for change, save in relation to presidents. Union presidents are often ceremonial positions with limited functions (such as chairing meetings of the executive) and there seems no justification for the law to impose the burden that they be elected by postal ballot of the entire membership if a union's rules provide, say, that the president be elected from amongst the executive members.

## Admission and discipline

6.9 Another area where the law has encroached on the right of trade union members to decide their own rules is in relation to admission and disciplining of members. Here UK law has prescribed that unions cannot exclude workers (including refusing admission) except on prescribed grounds and cannot discipline members for a number of specified offences – including for a refusal to participate in industrial action. This latter provision has been condemned by the international law bodies and disciplining of breakers of a lawful strike should be permitted to unions whose rules make this a disciplinary offence. Of course, the law should continue to insist that unions comply with their own disciplinary rules and that these are fair (ie. they comply with the rules of 'natural justice').

### Recommendations

i    *The statutory requirement that trade union presidents are elected by ballot of the whole membership be repealed.*

ii   *Unions should be free to decide their own admission and disciplinary rules (including the power, if the rulebook so provides, to discipline members who break lawful strikes and industrial action). This should be subject only to general laws such as those against impermissible discrimination.*

# The right of unions to have a legal status that enables them to defend themselves and carry out their functions effectively

6.10 In UK law unions are given a quasi-corporate status which, by and large, does not cause major problems save that the courts have held that unions, unlike companies, do not have sufficient legal status to sue for defamation. This seems an unjustified limitation on unions' rights to protect themselves from defamatory comments in the media and elsewhere. There are also special rules relating to trade union amalgamations and transfers of engagements. These seem to work adequately and do not seem to impose illegitimate burdens on unions.

### Recommendation
*iii.  Unions should be given the right to sue for defamation.*

# The right of unions to raise funds and to spend them as they see fit

## Trustees

6.11  The State has significantly encroached on trade union self-determination here. Unions must hold their assets through trustees – but this causes few problems, except that the judges have developed a special law of 'receivership' in relation to trade unions to allow trustees to be displaced by court appointed accountants if there is suspicion of a breach of the financial rules. It would be more consistent with international law if a trustee was in such circumstances replaced only by another member of the union and only after proof that the trustee breached or permitted a breach of the union's financial rules.

## Political funds

6.12  If unions in the UK wish to spend their money on political purposes they must ballot their members to decide to have a separate political fund. The rules of the union must then provide that members have a right not to contribute to the fund. These are objectionable interferences in trade union autonomy, though the principles seem, some 90 years after their introduction, to be accepted by the unions. What is regarded as an imposition is the requirement of the law that the union re-ballots every 10 years. This is very costly and former State finance for it has been withdrawn. Companies too are now required to ballot regularly for approval from shareholders to make political donations or incur political expenditure. But what is uniquely unfair to unions is that the regular re-balloting is imposed in tandem with the individual member's statutory right to opt out of paying into the political fund established by the ballot. On the principles of equality and proportionality, trade union law should be amended by removing the right of opt-out so that after a ballot in favour of the political fund (as on other matters) the minority are bound by the decision of the majority. Alternatively company law should add a shareholder's right to opt-out so that his or her share of the political fund is paid back in the form of extra dividend. But perhaps the easiest way to achieve justice here is to simply remove the burden of repeated political fund ballots from unions. This would conform to the traditional union democratic practice that once a policy is adopted it remains until such time as there is a call for it to be reversed or amended and the body which made the decision heeds the call and reverses or amends the policy.

## Financial records

6.13 Unions are required to place all their financial records (including those of branches) at the disposal of any member and his or her accountant on request. Transparency is an important principle but this is a heavy burden and has been exploited by malicious members intent on disrupting their union. Where an enquiring member can show he or she is acting in good faith and for good reason, the right to inspect the financial records of a union should remain. But where those qualifications cannot be proved, the burden of disclosure should be restricted to the annual accounts which the law requires every union to have audited by independent auditors (so that members of unions have similar rights to company shareholders). It should be remembered that the Certification Officer must be provided annually with each union's annual return and auditor's report and that the Certification Officer has formidable powers to appoint inspectors to investigate union finances and to require a union to produce any document he wishes to see.

## Indemnification

6.14 Unions, and no other body or person, are barred by law from using their funds to pay off ('indemnify') a fine imposed on a member by the courts. This should be removed so that the union and its rulebook is the arbiter of whether such a use of the union's funds can be made.

### Recommendations

iv   *The courts should only be permitted to replace a union trustee by a trustee appointed from the members of the union and only on proof that the replaced trustee permitted a breach of financial rules.*

v   *The requirement of repeated political fund ballots should be removed from trade unions.*

vi   *A union member's right to inspect financial records other than the annual accounts of a union should be qualified by a requirement on the enquiring member to prove that he or she is acting in good faith and has good reason for inspection of the particular records in question.*

vii   *The prohibition on a trade union from using its funds to indemnify a member in respect of a fine imposed on him or her should be repealed.*

# The right of unions to determine their own activities – industrial action

6.15 In this country, trade unions do not suffer any significant restrictions on the activities their members would wish them to carry out, save in two respects. One restriction is, of course, in relation to industrial action. The other is in relation to representation by a union of its members (this aspect is dealt with in chapter 7).

6.16 The right to take industrial action is a right of the individual worker; the right to organise industrial action is a right of a trade union as well as an individual right. These rights are fundamental human rights and must be protected as international law requires. But again, they are not rights without limits; and the permissible limits on industrial action have been well established by the international legal bodies. In this field, regrettably, UK law is consistently in breach of its international obligations.

6.17 The most noticeable failure of UK law is the absence of the right to strike found in most civilised jurisdictions. The consequences of there not being a right to strike in the UK are profound and are explored below. Apart from anything else the absence of a right to take industrial action has led to UK law having become so complex that the ILO has suggested only the implementation of a right to strike can simplify it.

## Industrial action and the worker

6.18 In UK law all forms of industrial action constitute a breach of an individual worker's contract of employment, either because industrial action amounts to a refusal to carry out the work which the contract requires the worker to carry out, or because it breaches the implied obligation not to seek to disrupt or injure the employer's business. Such a breach entitles the employer to dismiss the worker. The dismissed worker has a limited right to claim unfair dismissal (with no guarantee of reinstatement, even if ordered) if those on industrial action are selectively dismissed or selectively re-engaged within three months or where they are all sacked within eight weeks.

6.19 The rule that lawful industrial action constitutes a breach of contract justifying dismissal has been thoroughly condemned as being in breach of the ILO Conventions, the Council of Europe's Social Charter and the International Covenant on Economic, Social and Cultural Rights 1966. In most European countries a lawful strike does not break, but merely suspends, the contract of employment. It is therefore unlawful to sack a worker on lawful strike and the courts will prevent it. If this were the law here there would be no need for complex unfair dismissal rules to protect strikers. If a lawful strike suspended the contract of employment, there would be a need for incidental rules dealing with incidental matters, such as pay, pensions, seniority, holidays, unrelated misconduct, redundancy, replacement labour and so on.

---

## The International Covenant on Economic, Social and Cultural Rights and UK law

The Committee considers that failure to incorporate the right to strike into domestic law constitutes a breach of Article 8 of the Covenant. The Committee considers that the common law approach recognising only the freedom to strike, and the concept that strike action constitutes a fundamental breach of contract justifying dismissal, is not consistent with protection of the right to strike. The Committee does not find satisfactory the proposal to enable employees who go on strike to have a remedy before a tribunal for unfair dismissal. Employees participating in a lawful strike could not *ipso facto* be regarded as having committed a breach of an employment contract...

The Committee recommends that the right to strike be established in legislation, and that strike action does not entail any more the loss of employment, and it expresses the view that the current notion of freedom to strike, which simply recognises the illegality of being submitted to an involuntary servitude, is insufficient to satisfy the requirements of Article 8 of the Covenant...

*UN Committee on Economic, Social and Cultural Rights, December 1997*

---

6.20 Since industrial action breaches the contract of employment the worker is not entitled to be paid for time whilst taking industrial action. This would obviously equally apply if the contract were suspended during the action. But nowadays employers often deduct from wages on an unfair daily basis where the sum deducted is more than the worker would have earned had he or she performed all their duties that day.

## Industrial action and the trade union

6.21 The fact that participation in industrial action constitutes a breach of a worker's contract of employment is at the heart of contemporary legal controls on industrial action. This is because (as has been the case since the end of the 19th century) organising a strike and most other forms of industrial action constitutes the tort (civil wrong) of inducing another to act in breach of contract. This tort is the creation of the common law, that is law made by judges rather than Parliament, and a trade union and/or trade unionist committing this tort can be sued for damages. Most significantly, an

---

employer can get an injunction to prevent the commission of this tort, and, typically, these injunctions are interim in nature and are granted without a full court hearing. Violation of an injunction constitutes civil contempt and can result in the imposition of fines, imprisonment and sequestration. Related to this is the tort of interference with a commercial contract. This tort is generally committed when a trade union asks members employed by suppliers or customers of an employer in dispute, or employees of an associated company owned by the latter, to boycott goods or services destined for or provided by the employer in dispute. Workers in dispute who participate in peaceful picketing which is successful in persuading other workers not to cross a picket line will generally be committing both of these torts.

## Statutory restrictions

6.22 So, in the absence of a positive right to strike, the organisation of industrial action by a union (or individuals) is unlawful in the UK except to the extent of statutory immunity against these and other judge-made torts. In the past the judges have invented new torts to outflank the statutory immunities. However, a series of Acts introduced by Conservative governments between 1980 and 1993 has so reduced the statutory immunities that this particular problem has declined in practical importance. It has been the legislative whittling away of the statutory immunities that has led to the findings of the international bodies that UK law is in fundamental violation of international law. Today, industrial action only attracts statutory immunity if it is in contemplation or furtherance of a dispute that is 'wholly or mainly related' to terms and conditions of employment, or to other matters specified in the legislation such as job losses, disciplinary issues and trade union recognition/derecognition. If, according to a court, a union's predominant motive is outside the statutory 'trade dispute' issues, for example if it is held to be 'political', then immunity will be lost. This is contrary to international law which stipulates that industrial action is not to be confined to disputes with employers and is, in particular, to be permitted on matters of economic and social policy.

6.23 Under current UK law moreover, a 'trade dispute' must be between workers and their own employer. If the relevant dispute is between another employer and its workers then it is unlawful for a union to call for solidarity (sometimes referred to as secondary) action. The ILO and the Council of Europe have condemned this blanket ban. The ILO holds that solidarity action should be permissible if the primary action it is intended to support is lawful.

Furthermore, workers taking such action do not have any rights to unfair dismissal protection. This applies to a worker refusing to cross a picket line (see below). Employers have exploited this provision by dividing up business operations between a network of associated companies, or hiving off aspects of a business to another operator. There may of course be circumstances where workers do not want their trade union to act in a particular way, and in particular may not want their trade union to assist another group of workers. But the requirement of trade union freedom and autonomy means that the internal affairs of an organisation should be left to that organisation to resolve within the terms of its own rules. In particular it should not be open to outsiders such as employers to intervene through the courts on an issue of trade union democracy.

## The ILO, Convention 87 and the Right to Strike

The Committee has always considered that the right to strike is one of the essential means available to workers and their organisations for the promotion and protection of their economic and social interests as guaranteed by Articles 3, 8 and 10 of the Convention [87]. It has also taken the view that restrictions relating to the objectives of a strike and to the methods used should be sufficiently reasonable as not to result in practice in an excessive limitation of the exercise of the right to strike...

The current version of the 'immunities' is to be found in the Trade Union and Labour Relations Act 1974. The scope of these protections has been narrowed in a number of respects since 1980. The Committee notes, for example, that section 15 of the 1974 Act has been amended so as to limit the right to picket to a worker's own place of work or, in the case of a trade union official, the place of work of the relevant membership, whilst section 17 of the 1980 Act removes protection from 'secondary action' in the sense of action directed against an employer who is not directly a party to the given dispute. In addition, the definition of 'trade dispute' in section 29 of the 1974 Act has been narrowed so as to encompass only disputes between workers and their own employer, rather than disputes between 'employers and workers' or 'workers and workers' as was formerly the case.

Taken together, these changes appear to make it virtually impossible for workers and unions lawfully to engage in any form of boycott activity, or 'sympathetic' action against parties not directly involved in a given dispute. ...it appears to the Committee that where a boycott relates directly to the social and economic interests of the workers involved in either or both of the original dispute and the secondary action, and where the original dispute and the secondary action are not unlawful in themselves, then that boycott should be regarded as a legitimate exercise of the right to strike This is clearly consistent with the approach the Committee has adopted in relation to 'sympathy strikes'.

The Committee considers that a general prohibition of sympathy strikes could lead to abuse and that workers should be able to take such action provided the initial strike they are supporting is itself lawful.

Other changes to the definition of 'trade dispute' in the 1974 Act also appear to impose excessive limitations upon the exercise of the right to strike: (i) the definition now requires that the subject-matter of a dispute must relate 'wholly or mainly' to one or more of the matters set out in the definition – formerly it was sufficient that there be a 'connection' between the dispute and the specified matters. This change appears to deny protection to disputes where unions and their members have 'mixed' motives (for example, where they are pursuing both 'industrial' and 'political' or 'social' objectives). The Committee also considers that it would often be very difficult for unions to determine in advance whether any given course of conduct would, or would not, be regarded as having the necessary relation to the protected purposes; (ii) the fact that the definition now refers only to disputes between workers and 'their' employer could make it impossible for unions to take effective action in situations where the 'real' employer with whom they were in dispute was able to take refuge behind one or more subsidiary companies who were technically the 'employer' of the workers concerned, but who lacked the capacity to take decisions which are capable of satisfactorily resolving the dispute; and (iii) disputes relating to matters outside the United Kingdom can now be protected only where the persons whose actions in the United Kingdom are said to be in contemplation or furtherance of a trade dispute relating to matters occurring outside the United Kingdom are likely to be affected in respect of one or more of the protected matters by the outcome of the dispute. This means that there would be no protection for industrial action which was intended to protect or to improve the terms and conditions of employment of workers outside the United Kingdom, or to register disapproval of the social or racial policies of a government with whom the United Kingdom had trading or economic links. The Committee has consistently taken the view that strikes that are purely political in character do not fall within the scope of the principles of freedom of association. However, it also considers that trade unions ought to have the possibility of recourse to protest strikes, in particular where aimed at criticising a government's economic and social policies... The revised definition of 'trade dispute' appears to deny workers that right.

The Committee considers that the overall effect of legislative change in this area since 1980 is to withdraw protection from strikes and other forms of industrial action in circumstances where such action ought to be permissible in order to enable workers and their unions adequately to protect and to promote their economic and social interests, and to organise their activities... Accordingly, it would ask the government to introduce amendments which enable workers to take industrial action against their "real" employer and which accord adequate protection of the right to engage in other legitimate forms of industrial action such as protest strikes and sympathy strikes, as guaranteed by Articles 3, 8 and 10 of the Convention.

*The ILO Committee of Experts, approved by the ILO in 1994*

6.24 Because of the bar on secondary action, a worker may only picket his or her own place of work even though, as in the Wapping dispute in 1986, the employer is no longer based there. This is contrary to international law as the ILO and the Council of Europe have declared. With freedom of assembly now guaranteed by the Human Rights Act pickets should be freely entitled to assemble and peacefully to attempt to persuade people not to cross the picket line.

## Picketing and Freedom of Assembly

The freedom to strike is an essential part of the right of workers to bargain collectively with their employers. The organisation of a picket is, in turn, an essential part of the freedom to strike. But industrial pickets are also a particular form of the use of a general right, the right to assemble peacefully...Virtually all industrial action is now at the mercy of the courts... a trade unionist standing peacefully outside someone else's workplace in a gesture of solidarity with those on strike may be ordered by the courts to leave and, if he refuses to do so, may be imprisoned... The use of ...injunctions is an obvious and unjustified denial of freedom of assembly and communication . But the law is not simply destructive of people's right to assemble and make their views known. Economic torts and the labour injunction are the chief weapons of private property against labour; they are perhaps the most naked example of the real interests of the law. The courts will readily protect an employer against a threat to his business: they will not protect an employee against the loss of his livelihood. They will not even defend the only means available to workers – collective industrial action.

*Patricia Hewitt, The Abuse of Power (1982)*

6.25 The Conservative legislation, preserved by the present government imposed many further restrictions on industrial action of which space does not permit consideration. Examples are:

● Industrial action to seek the reinstatement of workers dismissed for taking unofficial action is unlawful;
● Industrial action to enforce union negotiated rates of pay and

conditions through a union recognition requirement to be incorporated into contracts for goods and services is unlawful;

- The Prison Officers' Association is barred from taking industrial action, though this is contrary to international law.

With the implementation of the right to strike into UK law such infringements of the right to strike should be repealed.

## Ballots and notices

6.26 Even where industrial action falls within the narrow statutory definition of a trade dispute, immunity will still be lost by a trade union if it fails to comply with highly complex procedures requiring a fully postal industrial action ballot. Furthermore, pre-ballot and pre-strike notices in due form must be sent to the employer in dispute in accordance with a strict timetable. These complicated technical requirements have imposed huge (and otherwise unnecessary) burdens on union record keeping, and have meant that minor and unintended failures have enabled employers to obtain injunctions to stop the industrial action. Whilst a legal requirement for pre-industrial action ballots does not breach international law, and is something that unions have accepted in this country, the procedural requirements surrounding these ballots and notices are such as to impair the right to organise lawful industrial action and confer protection on those taking it. The government itself conceded to this to the ILO but the changes so far brought about by legislation in 1999 have not achieved the right to strike in compliance with international law.

---

### Trade Union Democracy Undermined

In *London Underground v RMT* in 2001, the union, after an overwhelming ballot in favour of strike action, gave notice specifying the number of members and described them as being "all RMT members employed by London Underground Limited in all workplaces." The employer complained that this was not sufficient to comply with the requirement of the Employment Relations Act 1999. The courts agreed. Information held by the union meant held by "any official of RMT who, in accordance with RMT's rules and normal operating procedures, was concerned with maintaining records kept for RMT's purposes." Such information as these officials possessed as to the number, category or workplace of the employees concerned, should have been given to the employer to enable the latter "to make plans," ie. strike breaking plans.

---

6.27 It is necessary to remove the technicalities of pre-strike ballots and to remove the requirement of notices altogether. The reasons for and the circumstances of industrial action vary enormously. It should be for the workers and their unions to decide how best to ascertain their collective views. This would not prevent dissatisfied members from challenging their unions in the courts if the union's rules were breached but no employer should have the right to intervene on such grounds. Workplace ballots might be more suitable in some circumstances, and in emergency situations the ballot might have to come after the industrial action had started – eg. where an employer imposed a unilateral change to terms and conditions of employment or announced redundancies without consultation or sacked a shop steward. Indeed, where workers spontaneously walk out in such circumstances there would appear to be no need to ballot them as well. What is required is that unions should have appropriate rules to ensure that decisions to take industrial action are made by members democratically. The Certification Officer could check for this on a regular basis.

6.28 International law on trade union autonomy does not, in particular, permit employers relying solely on the ground of some irregularity in trade union democratic decision making, to interfere in a trade union decision to take industrial action: such a complaint is for the members alone to take up.

6.29 A further issue arises when a worker not involved in a dispute is asked not to cross a picket line by workers who are taking industrial action. If he or she decides out of principle not to cross the picket line then he or she is taking industrial action and so his or her contract of employment should be treated as suspended but there should be no obligation on a union that he or she (or all persons who might be asked not to cross a picket line) be balloted. The decision whether or not to cross a picket line is an individual decision which should not require a ballot to save a union from being sued.

## Injunctions

6.30 A further problem in industrial action law is the use of the interlocutory injunction. This emergency procedure (and injunctions against industrial action are always emergencies) does not require the claimant (usually the employer) to prove the facts alleged either beyond all reasonable doubt or on the balance of probabilities: it is sufficient to assert facts which, so long as they appear credible, will be accepted by the Court, notwithstanding that the union has evidence to the contrary. The employer need not even demonstrate that its case is stronger than the union's. It is enough to show "a serious issue to be tried". If credible facts are asserted and an arguable case on the law demonstrated, the Court will grant an injunction if the "balance of convenience" favours it. In practice the Court will almost invariably grant an injunction to stop the industrial action unless the union shows the employer's legal argument is unsustainable, since the balance of convenience invariably tilts towards protecting the employer (and, it is usually alleged, the public) from the inconvenience of the industrial action.

---

It is open to an employer to seek an interlocutory injunction in cases where a strike may be unlawful and that such an injunction may be granted provided the employer can show that there is a case to answer, without the court deciding the issue on the merits. Thus, any removal of "immunities" provides for more situations where a strike may be halted, quickly, reducing the effectiveness of the right to strike in achieving collective agreement.

*The Council of Europe's Committee of Experts, 1992*

---

The common law renders virtually all forms of strikes or other industrial action unlawful as a matter of civil law. This means that workers and unions who engage in such action are liable to be sued for damages by employers (or other parties) who suffer loss as a consequence, and (more importantly in practical terms) may be restrained from committing unlawful acts by means of injunctions (issued on both an interlocutory and a permanent basis). It appears to the Committee that unrestricted access to such remedies would deny workers the right to take strikes or other industrial action in order to protect and to promote their economic and social interests.

*The ILO Committee of Experts approved by the ILO in 1994*

## Recommendations

viii  *Every worker should have the right to take industrial action.*

ix  *Every trade union should have the right to organise, encourage and support industrial action by its members.*

x  *These rights should be subject only to those limitations recognised by international law.*

xi  *The law should provide that lawful industrial action does not constitute a breach of the contract of employment but merely suspends the contract.*

xii  *Any dismissal of a worker taking lawful industrial action or by reason that she took or intended to take industrial action should be void.*

xiii  *A worker taking industrial action should not be penalised by losing*

---

*more than the sum that he or she would have earned had they not taken industrial action.*

xiv *The right to take industrial action should extend to taking industrial action as a means of resolving any dispute which relates to the workers' interests at work; this should include the economic and social matters on which a trade union has a policy.*

xv *Solidarity industrial action should be lawful, provided that it is intended to support lawful primary industrial action.*

xvi *A worker should have the right to peacefully assemble and picket at locations other than his or her own place of work.*

xvii *All UK restrictions on the right to take industrial action should be repealed save for those explicitly permitted by the supervisory bodies of the ILO and the Council of Europe's Social Charter.*

xviii *The obligation to serve pre-ballot and pre-strike notices should be abolished.*

xix *Though union rules should make provision for ballots before industrial action, unions should be free to ballot at the workplace or by post or, in emergencies, not at all.*

xx *No employer should have the right to complain to a court that a trade union has failed to ballot or ballot properly before industrial action.*

xxi *Refusal to cross or an invitation not to cross a picket line should not require a ballot in order to be lawful.*

xxii *No injunction should be granted to restrain industrial action without a full trial.*

# Conclusion

## The right of unions to determine their own rulebook and constitution free from State and employer interference

i    The statutory requirement that trade union presidents are elected by ballot of the whole membership be repealed.

ii   Unions should be free to decide their own admission and disciplinary rules (including the power, if the rulebook so provides, to discipline members who break lawful strikes and industrial action). This should be subject only to general laws such as those against impermissible discrimination.

## The right of unions to have a legal status that enables them to defend themselves and carry out their functions effectively

iii  Unions should be given the right to sue for defamation.

## The right of unions to raise funds and to spend them as they see fit

iv   The courts should only be permitted to replace a union trustee by a trustee appointed from the members of the union and only on proof that the replaced trustee permitted a breach of financial rules.

v    The requirement of repeated political fund ballots should be removed from trade unions.

vi   A union member's right to inspect financial records other than the annual accounts of a union should be qualified by a requirement on the enquiring member to prove that he or she is acting in good faith and has good reason for inspection of the particular records in question.

vii  The prohibition on a trade union from using its funds to indemnify a member in respect of a fine imposed on him or her should be repealed.

## The right of unions to determine their own activities – industrial action

viii Every worker should have the right to take industrial action.

ix    Every trade union should have the right to organise, encourage and support industrial action by its members.

x    These rights should be subject only to those limitations recognised by international law.

xi    The law should provide that lawful industrial action does not constitute a breach of the contract of employment but merely suspends the contract.

xii    Any dismissal of a worker taking lawful industrial action or by reason that she took or intended to take industrial action should be void.

xiii    A worker taking industrial action should not be penalised by losing more than the sum that he or she would have earned had they not taken industrial action.

xiv    The right to take industrial action should extend to taking industrial action as a means of resolving any dispute which relates to the workers' interests at work; this should include the economic and social matters on which a trade union has a policy.

xv    Solidarity industrial action should be lawful, provided that it is intended to support lawful primary industrial action.

xvi    A worker should have the right to peacefully assemble and picket at locations other than his or her own place of work.

xvii    All UK restrictions on the right to take industrial action should be repealed save for those explicitly permitted by the supervisory bodies of the ILO and the Council of Europe's Social Charter.

xviii    The obligation to serve pre-ballot and pre-strike notices should be abolished.

xix    Though union rules should make provision for ballots before industrial action, unions should be free to ballot at the workplace or by post or, in emergencies, not at all.

xx    No employer should have the right to complain to a court that a trade union has failed to ballot or ballot properly before industrial action.

xxi    Refusal to cross or an invitation not to cross a picket line should not require a ballot in order to be lawful.

xxii    No injunction should be granted to restrain industrial action without a full trial.

# Chapter 7

# Trade union rights in the workplace

7.1 One vital principle which must be central to any Workers' Charter is the right to collective bargaining. This right is acknowledged by all relevant international laws, including ILO Convention 98 and the Council of Europe's Social Charter, to both of which the United Kingdom is a party. The restoration of collective bargaining is the central means of achieving a balance of power, democracy, participation, justice and dignity in the workplace. Yet the changes to labour law over the last twenty years or so have seriously undermined collective bargaining to the extent that the United Kingdom has the lowest proportion of its workforce covered by a collective agreement than any country in Europe. Indeed Britain is the only EC member state where less than half of the workforce has the protection of a collective agreement, and one of only a few countries where employers are not required to consult about major changes to working conditions.

7.2 How can this be? The New Labour government introduced new rights for workers and trade unions in the Employment Relations Act 1999. These included,

- The right of workers to be accompanied (but not represented) in grievance and disciplinary cases;
- The right of trade unions to apply to the CAC for recognition where they have the support of a majority of the workers in an approved bargaining unit.

These measures are extremely important. The first allows unions access to workers and workplaces where they would otherwise be excluded. The second has been responsible for a large number of voluntary recognition agreements which have been concluded in the shadow of the law. Unions are able to demonstrate support and employers are aware that a voluntary agreement is better than one concluded through the complex statutory procedure. According to the TUC, no fewer then 50 voluntary agreements were being struck each month by the time the legislation was a year old. But although these are significant advances, this legislation does not go far enough to meet the reasonable claims of trade unions and their members, and a number of other legal changes are needed to make the right to collective bargaining a reality. The changes required are considered in this and the following chapter.

## A right to be represented by a trade union

7.3 So far as the statutory right of a worker to be accompanied in grievance and disciplinary proceedings is concerned, there are two major problems here. One is that it is a right to be accompanied, and not a right to be represented, though the companion is entitled to address the hearing, but not answer questions on behalf of the employee. This limitation was strongly criticised at the time it was introduced, though in practice it is unclear whether the gap between the right to be accompanied and the right to be represented is as wide as had been feared. But if there are lingering doubts these need to be clarified, particularly after the implementation of the Employment Act 2002 by which workers in unfair dismissal cases will be penalised for not having first used workplace procedures to resolve a dispute with their employer. In these circumstances it becomes even more important that the worker is properly represented in disciplinary and grievance proceedings, and that there is an 'equality of arms' between the parties. This is a matter to which we return in chapter 9 below. But for the present, the legislation should make clear that a worker has a right to be *represented* in grievance or disciplinary proceedings by a trade union official or another person of his or her choice.

7.4 The other concern about the right to be accompanied is that it applies in the case of grievances only in relation to *existing* terms and conditions of employment: that is to say to grievance hearings which concern the performance of a 'duty by an employer in relation to a worker'. In the *Code of Practice on Disciplinary and Grievance Procedures* (2000), it is stated that this means a 'legal duty arising from statute or common law', which means that there is no right to be accompanied where the grievance relates to a complaint that wages are too low, that working time is excessive, or that an application for promotion has failed, unless in each case it is possible to claim that the employer is in breach of some statutory obligation (such as the National Minimum Wage Act 1998, the Working Time Regulations 1998, or the Sex Discrimination Act 1975). But the Code of Practice makes it clear that the right to be accompanied at a grievance hearing would generally not apply to 'an individual's request for a pay rise', 'grievances about the application of a grading or promotion exercise', or 'grievances arising out of day to day friction between fellow workers', unless the friction develops into incidents of bullying or harassment. No justification has ever been provided for these limitations, and the legislation should be amended to make it clear that the right to representation applies to all matters relating to the employment relationship.

### Recommendations

i    *Workers should have a right to be represented in grievance or disciplinary proceedings by a trade union official or by another person of their choice, and to be given a reasonable opportunity during working time to consult the representative and prepare for the hearing.*

ii   *The right to representation should apply to all matters relating to the employment relationship. It should not be confined to discipline or grievances about existing duties of the employer. A worker seeking to renegotiate the terms of his or her contract should be entitled to be represented when doing so.*

# The right of collective representation: filling the legislative gap

7.5  The second problem with the existing legislation is the chasm between the right to be accompanied in disciplinary and grievance proceedings, and the right to recognition for the purposes of collective bargaining. This means that a substantial number of workers in a workplace could be in a trade union, yet be denied by their employer of any form of representation by their trade union.

---

## NUM and Hatfield Coal Company

The NUM applied for statutory recognition, claiming that 29 per cent of the workers in the bargaining unit were members of the union. The CAC ruled the application inadmissible, the union unable to satisfy the CAC that a majority of workers in the bargaining unit would support recognition. So even though the union had almost a third of the workforce in membership, it was unable even to have a ballot on recognition,

---

> with the result that the union members were denied a collective voice at the workplace.

There can be no justification for denying a collective voice to workers in such circumstances, which appears to be in breach of the ECHR. This was made clear by the European Court of Human Rights in *Wilson and Palmer v United Kingdom* (2002).

> "The ...essence of a voluntary system of collective bargaining is that it must be possible for a trade union which is not recognised by an employer to take steps including, if necessary, organising industrial action, with a view to persuading the employer to enter into collective bargaining with it on those issues which the union believes are important for its members' interests. Furthermore, it is of the essence of the right to join a trade union for the protection of their interests that employees should be free to instruct or permit the union to make representations to their employer or to take action in support of their interests on their behalf. If workers are prevented from so doing, their freedom to belong to a trade union, for the protection of their interests, become illusory. It is the role of the State to ensure that trade union members are not prevented or restrained from using their union to represent them in attempts to regulate their relations with their employers."
>
> *Wilson and Palmer v United Kingdom* (2002)

Where a trade union does not have a majority in membership in a particular workplace to qualify for recognition under the statutory procedure, **individual workers should have the right to be collectively represented by their trade union.** It would then be for the employer to decide whether to extend terms negotiated in this way to non union members. But it should not be possible for an employer to treat non trade union members more favourably than those of his or her workforce who are trade union members.

7.6 A measure of this kind would bring the United Kingdom into closer compliance not only with the ECHR, but also with its obligation under international law to take measures appropriate to national conditions to 'encourage and promote the full development' of collective bargaining machinery. This obligation – derived from ILO Convention 98 on the Right to Organise and Collective Bargaining, 1949, and re-affirmed by the United Kingdom and by the other countries of the world in the ILO Declaration on Fundamental Principles and Rights At Work, 1998 – is not qualified by a codicil which says that it applies only where a majority of the workers so require. Indeed the ILO supervisory bodies have stated time and again that where recognition is dependent upon majority support, steps must also be taken to allow trade unions to bargain on behalf of their members, even though they are in a minority. This does not mean of course that a minority union could cut across the rights of an established union which is recognised by the employer. It is important to emphasise that any new right to bargain on behalf of members should apply only where there is no other trade union which is recognised by the employer, either voluntarily or under the statutory procedure.

### Recommendations

iii    *Where an independent trade union does not have a majority in membership in a particular workplace to qualify for recognition under the statutory procedure, individual workers should have the right to be collectively represented by their independent trade union.*

iv    *A right of workers to be represented collectively by an independent trade union should apply only where there is no other independent trade union which is recognised by the employer for the workforce as a whole, either voluntarily or under the statutory procedure. Where there is a recognised union, representational rights should be exercised only by that union.*

# The right to trade union recognition: a need for revision

7.7 The statutory procedure has helped to stimulate recognition by voluntary agreements where there is sufficient support from the workforce. Most applications made to the CAC under the procedure succeed in establishing admissibility; and in most cases that continue beyond that stage, the unions are usually able to demonstrate majority membership or majority support in a ballot. Moreover, the procedure has been impressively impervious to judicial review, unlike the earlier procedure in the 1970s. Indeed in those cases which have been the subject of judicial review, the applications have ultimately failed, the courts showing in two leading cases a remarkable deference to the CAC in circumstances where they might have been expected to have intervened in the past.

7.8 But this is not to say that there is no room for revision and reform, or no room for improvement. Some of the flaws deliberately tailored into the legislation make it impossible in some cases and more difficult in others to realise the government's stated aim that trade unions should have a right to be recognised in accordance with the wishes of a majority of the workforce. Some of these problems have been highlighted in a number of cases in the CAC in which the unions have failed, despite having majority membership in their proposed bargaining units. Difficulties relate specifically to the fact that

- the procedure does not apply unless the employer (together with an associated employer) employs more than 20 workers. This excludes some 5 million workers in small firms from the procedure, and in doing so appears to be inconsistent with international obligations which do not distinguish between employers on the basis of the number of people they employ. It also gives rise to the anomaly that 12 union members in a company of 22 workers can get statutory recognition, but that 20 in a company of 20 cannot.

---

## GPMU and Keely Print

GPMU made an application for recognition against Keely Print. The question for the CAC was whether the application was valid, in the sense that the company employed more than 20 people. The answer depended on whether a director of the company was also an employee of the company. The CAC held he was not, and the application was rejected. The union could not use the procedure.

---

- an application can be blocked where there is an existing agreement with a non independent trade union. This is in clear breach of Britain's obligations under international law, and is unparalleled in countries such as the USA and Canada where such anti-union devices are unlawful. Under the Employment Relations Act 1999 an agreement with a non independent union may block an application by an independent union, even though the 'agreement' does not cover pay, hours or holidays.

---

## Prison Officers' Association and Securicor

The POA made an application under the procedure for recognition against Securicor in relation to a prison in South Wales. The company had already 'recognised' an in-house staff association which was not an independent trade union. Even though a majority of the workers were members of the POA, the application was ruled inadmissible on the ground that the employer already recognised another trade union.

---

- an application can fail even though the union has a majority in membership because the proposed bargaining unit is not 'compatible with effective management'. This requirement of the legislation is used by employers to expand bargaining units proposed by unions in order to dilute union strength. Employers will seek to expand the categories of workers to be included in the unit, or in

---

the case of an employer operating from several sites, seek to expand the number of sites to include locations where the union has no current strength.

## Hygena and ISTC

The ISTC sought recognition for all manual shopfloor workers (with a number of exceptions) employed at the company's Scunthorpe division. The company resisted the application on the ground that the bargaining unit should cover all six of its plants throughout the country, amounting to 2,134 manual workers and 84 supervisors. This was said by the company to be an established group of employees currently managed as one unit, all covered by the same terms and conditions of employment. This was accepted by the CAC which ruled that the bargaining unit proposed by the union was not compatible with effective management.

7.9 But although these may be the three most notorious difficulties, there are others. Thus, (i) a trade union which has a majority membership may still be required under the legislation to have a recognition ballot, adding further to the delay in the procedure; (ii) trade unions have no statutory right of access to the workforce until the beginning of the balloting period, thereby giving the employer an opportunity to bring pressure to bear on workers from the date of the application until the date of the ballot; (iii) where a ballot is held, trade unions must obtain the support not only of a majority of those voting in the ballot but also 40 per cent of those eligible to vote. In addition, recognition is confined to collective bargaining on a narrow range of issues (pay, hours and holidays), though it is true that once recognised a union will also acquire a number of consultation rights. Nevertheless the limitations have been exposed by a CAC decision about whether pay includes pensions. There should be no room for doubt about such matters, with a more extensive collective bargaining agenda set out more clearly in the legislation. Concerns are also raised by the punitive provision which bars a union from bringing an application within three years of an unsuccessful application. While some limitation of this kind might be justified for a number of reasons, three years is too long.

### Recommendation

v   *The statutory procedure should be revised in order to promote the objective set out in the White Paper Fairness at Work. The revisions should specifically:*
    *(a) remove the restriction that the procedure applies only to employers*

---

*of more then 20 workers; (b) remove the ability of employers to defeat
applications under the procedure by granting 'recognition' to non
independent trade unions; (c) dilute the requirement that bargaining
units should be 'compatible with effective management'; (d) remove
the power of the CAC to order a ballot where the union has majority
membership; (e) remove the 40 per cent rule in a recognition ballot
whereby trade unions must demonstrate not only majority support but
also the support of at least 40 per cent of the workers in the
bargaining unit; (f) expand the range of collective bargaining issues
to which the procedure applies beyond pay, hours and holidays; and
(g) reduce to one year the waiting period before another application
can be made by the same union in respect of the same bargaining
unit.*

# The scourge of anti-unionism

## Discrimination against trade unionists

7.10 An issue which remains outstanding is the extent to which
British law permits employers to engage in various forms of anti
union activity. Remarkably, it continues to be possible for employers
to discriminate against trade unionists, in relation to terms and conditions of employment. This arise because of the decision in *Wilson v
Associated Newspapers plc* where the employer de-recognised the
union (the NUJ) and introduced personal contracts for staff who
were previously governed by a collective agreement. Those workers
who agreed in the future to have their terms and conditions governed by personal contracts would be paid more than those who
wished to have their terms and conditions governed by the collective
agreements in force at the time of the de-recognition. It was held by
the House of Lords that the protection against discrimination on the
ground of trade union membership did not apply where the reason
for discrimination was that the employee refused to have his terms
and conditions governed by a collective agreement rather than a personal contract. This decision is reinforced by the so called Ullswater
amendment (after the hapless minister responsible) introduced by
the previous Conservative government in 1993, authorising employers in some circumstances to discriminate against trade unionists on
matters such as pay.

7.11 In these two different ways anti-union discrimination is
expressly permissible in British law. British law is thus clearly in
breach of international law: it breaches ILO Convention 98 as well
as the Council of Europe's Social Charter of 1961. So far as the former is concerned, the ILO Committee of Experts has condemned

the current law as allowing an employer 'wilfully to discriminate on anti-union grounds', and as 'condoning anti-union discrimination'. It was also held decisively by the European Court of Human Rights in *Wilson and Palmer v United Kingdom* (2002) to violate article 11 of the ECHR.

> "by permitting employers to use financial incentives to induce employees to surrender important union rights, the respondent state failed in its positive obligation to secure the enjoyment of the rights under article 11 of the Convention. This failure amounted to a violation of article 11, as regards both the applicant unions and the individual applicants."
>
> *Wilson and Palmer v United Kingdom* (2002)

Steps to address the problem were made in the Employment Relations Act 1999 which enables the Secretary of State to make regulations about cases where a worker is subjected to a detriment or dismissed because he or she 'refuses to enter into a contract which includes terms which differ from the terms of a collective agreement' applicable to him or her. But this power has never been exercised, and in any event it is expressly provided that the payment of higher wages for agreeing to a personal contract (as in the *Wilson* case) is not to be regarded as a detriment. The measure is thus rather pointless, and there is a clear need for the government to return to the parliamentary drawing board before powers of this kind can be used.

## Unfair labour practices

7.12 More recently the statutory recognition procedure has seen the return of different forms of anti-union conduct by employers. Some employers now respond to the prospect of a trade union making a recognition application with a variety of tactics. These include the setting up of a works council to draw support from union organisers; the use of threats and intimidation (such as the threat to close the company); and the surveillance of workers who are approached by union officials. According to Roger Lyons:

"We need 10 per cent membership in any workplace to trigger a ballot for union recognition. Some anti-union employers are surrounding their staff with razor wire and high-tech surveillance equipment to make it impossible for trade unions to communicate with them."

Current law makes inadequate provision for dealing with employer conduct of this kind. Trade unions have a right of access to a workplace but only during a recognition ballot. Yet the need for access begins long before then, from at least the time an application is made to the CAC. *The Code of Practice on Access to Workers During Recognition and Derecognition Ballots* encourages employers and trade unions to avoid acrimonious situations and to behave responsibly. But this applies only during the balloting period under the statutory procedure, and is in any event not easily enforceable.

---

## Code of Practice on Access to Workers During Recognition and Derecognition Ballots

Both parties should endeavour to ensure that, wherever possible, potentially acrimonious situations are avoided throughout the period of access. In particular, the parties should avoid:

- using defamatory material or provocative propaganda;
- personal attacks or personalised negative campaigning against individuals;
- the harassment or intimidation of individuals;
- issuing threats;
- placing pressure on workers to reveal their voting intentions; and
- behaviour likely to cause unnecessary offence.

---

7.13 There is thus a need for measures to deal with hostile employer activity, particularly during the early stages of a union organisation campaign. There is currently legislation which makes it unlawful for employers to discriminate against or dismiss employees because of trade union membership or activities (subject to the qualification already referred to), or because of involvement in a statutory recognition campaign. But there is no effective regulation of employer conduct designed to disrupt trade union organisation activity by creating a hostile and intimidatory environment in order to discourage support for a union. One way of dealing with this would be make it unlawful as an unfair labour practice to engage in anti-union activity. This could be defined to include the conduct which is referred to in the first four bullet points of paragraph 43 of the *Code of Practice on Access to Workers During Recognition and Derecognition Ballots,* which should be unlawful, whenever the conduct in question takes place, and not only during a ballot. It should also include the surveillance of workers, and the refusal of an employer to allow a union official access to a workplace to communicate with any member who may be employed there. Trade unions should be entitled to enter any workplace at a reasonable time on giving notice to the employer to communicate with members employed there.

## Recommendations

vi  *The Ullswater amendment allowing employers to discriminate against trade unionists should be repealed, and it should be made clear in legislation that the protection from discrimination on the ground of trade union membership applies also to discrimination based on the use or enjoyment of trade union services, facilities or benefits. In particular it should be unlawful for an employer to subject any worker to a detriment in any respect on the ground that he or she refuses to enter into a contract which includes terms which differ from the terms of a collective agreement applicable to him or her.*

vii  *It should be an unfair labour practice for an employer to engage in any form of anti-union activity. The following conduct should be regarded as an unfair labour practice:*

- *surveillance of workers related to trade union membership or activities, or trade union recognition;*
- *using defamatory material or provocative propaganda;*
- *personal attacks or personalised negative campaigning against individuals;*
- *the harassment or intimidation of individuals;*
- *issuing threats;*
- *refusing a union access to the employer's premises to communicate with a member.*

*It should also be regarded as an unfair labour practice (in addition to any other remedy the law currently provides) to discriminate or dismiss workers because of their trade union membership or activities; or to refuse to co-operate with the CAC. Where an employer is found to have committed an unfair labour practice, the CAC should have the power (a) to impose a financial penalty on the employer; (b) to make an award of compensation to any workers affected; (c) to reinstate any worker who has been dismissed; (d) to waive where the circumstances so warrant any of the admissibility requirements for the bringing of an application under the statutory protection (such as the requirement of 10 per cent membership); (e) to permit a trade union to re-submit any unsuccessful application without the need to comply with the existing three year rule; and (f) where appropriate to award recognition without the need for a ballot.*

# Rights of recognised trade unions

## Existing rights

7.14  Under current legislation, trade unions acquire a number of statutory rights once recognised by an employer. Recognition for this purpose may be voluntary recognition, or recognition under the

statutory procedure. Once recognised
- a trade union is entitled to the disclosure of certain information by the employer where this is necessary for the purposes of collective bargaining
- trade union officials and members in the workplace are entitled to time off to enable them to carry out industrial relations duties and activities
- trade unions have the right to be informed and consulted about transfers of undertakings and about redundancies in the workplace.

In addition, where a union has been recognised under the statutory procedure, it has the right to be consulted on training matters, but there is no such right in the case of voluntary recognition.

## Time off and facilities

7.15 These measures are deficient in a number of ways, both in terms of the substance of the existing rights and the narrow range of matters which they cover. So far as the right to time off is concerned, there is evidence that trade unions are finding difficulty in ensuring that their members and officials are released in order to enable them to carry out their duties. Yet as available time is contracting, so the responsibilities of union officials at the workplace are increasing, with new legislation adding significantly to the burdens of union officials. There is a also a curious failure in the legislation to take the question of facilities seriously, an important matter which is relegated to a single paragraph of the *Code of Practice on Time Off for Trade Union Duties and Activities,* which encourages employers to 'consider making available to officials the facilities necessary for them to perform their duties efficiently'. At the present time there is no way by which a trade union can require an employer to enter into a reasonable facilities agreement, save only that a complaint may be made to an employment tribunal that the employer has refused reasonable time off in specific cases. Where a union is being denied reasonable facilities (including time off), it ought to be possible for a complaint to be made to the CAC which should have the power to determine a facilities agreement for the parties.

## Consultation on training

7.16 So far as other matters are concerned, there are two important gaps in terms of the rights of recognised trade unions. The first relates to training. Trade unions have a right to be consulted about training where they obtain recognition under the statutory procedure and a collective bargaining method has been specified by the

CAC, but not otherwise. It is not clear why only employers who are the subject of an order as to collective bargaining need to be the subject of this particular duty and others not. What are the special characteristics of these employers whose identity is unknown in advance? Why is it assumed that other employers are more likely to yield to a trade union request to be consulted on training? This distinction based upon the means by which collective bargaining is secured is irrational and silly. Legislation does not confine the rights of union learning representatives to those whose union is the subject of a statutory recognition order. Why is it any more sensible to confine the union's right to be consulted on training to such cases? The denial of consultation rights is all the more bizarre for the government's commitment to education and training as a way to higher productivity. The only conclusion to be drawn is that the government believes that trade unions have nothing usefully to add to the training agenda, except in the most unusual cases.

## Consultation on pensions

7.17 The other matter relates to pensions. An issue of great contemporary importance is the robbing of workers' security in retirement by the unilateral variation of their pension entitlement. There have been many examples recently of employers reducing the pension benefits payable on retirement of their workers. It should not be possible for an employer to vary the terms of an occupational pension scheme without first consulting and securing the agreement of a recognised trade union. (Where there is no recognised trade union, it should be necessary for the employer to consult and secure the agreement of the information and consultation body to be established under the Information and Consultation Directive, which is considered at paragraphs 7.18-7.21 below).

### Recommendations

viii   *A recognised trade union should have the right to refer a complaint to the CAC about time off and facilities provided to its workplace representatives by an employer. The CAC should be empowered to determine the content of an agreement which would be enforced in the event of breach, both in terms of time off and facilities, by employment tribunals.*

ix   *A recognised trade union should have the right to be consulted by the employer on matters relating to training at the workplace. Where there is no recognised trade union, employers should be required to consult with the information and consultation body established under the Information and Consultation Directive.*

x   *A recognised trade union should have the right to be consulted by an*
*employer before any change is made to the pension arrangements of*
*the workers in the bargaining unit. Where there is no recognised trade*
*union, employers should be required to consult with the information*
*and consultation body established under the Information and*
*Consultation Directive. There should be no right on the part of an*
*employer unilaterally to vary pension provisions.*

## Information, consultation and participation

7.18 Rice crispy redundancies are now widespread in Britain –
workers hear of their fate not directly from their employer or even
through their union, but at their breakfast through television, radio
or newspapers, sometimes as a result of an announcement to the
City. Recent high profile examples include Corus steel, Marks and
Spencer, Rover, Vauxhall, and Royal Mail. Another example is
Express Digital Media – on a Friday afternoon, the 46 staff were
made redundant when the company went into liquidation, a month
after having been sold to a new owner for £1. Staff posted a message
on the *Express Newspaper* website, saying 'This bears the hallmarks of
a cynical legal ploy to avoid paying staff any notice or redundancy
money'. It was quickly removed. Together these incidents are cruel
reminders of the limited rights of workers even in workplaces where
there is a recognised union.

7.19 All this should change with the implementation of the
Information and Consultation Directive. It is impossible to exagger-
ate the potential importance of this measure in the light of recent
employer behaviour. Apart from addressing these problems directly,
the Directive will provide trade unions with an opportunity to establish a stake in workplaces, and if implemented carefully, could com-
plement the trade union recognition procedures and thereby give
unions a stronger voice. The Directive will require the introduction
of legislation whereby employers of more than 50 workers (or in
some cases 20) will be required to provide information about the
business's activities, and consult about any measures which will
threaten employment, and about decisions likely to lead to substantial changes in work organisation or contractual relations. Failure to
comply with these obligations should be met by sanctions which are
'effective, proportionate and dissuasive'. These are minimum standards which can be improved upon and adapted to the British experience. But they need not be implemented in a grudging and minimalist way. The legislation should specify the purposes for which
information and consultation must take place.

7.20 There are nevertheless a number of concerns which will

have to be overcome if the full value of the Directive is to realised in the British context. The assumption is that it is to be an effective channel for the communication of information to workers' representatives, and an effective channel for worker consultation. The assumption therefore is that it is not to be defeated by cynical provisions designed to undermine these expectations. To this end, the legislation to implement the Directive should impose an obligation to inform and consult on all employers who employ more than 20 workers (or less if the trade union recognition threshold is reduced). Where there is a recognised trade union, this should be the body with which information and consultation takes place for the purposes of the Directive. And where there is no recognised trade union, all employers should be required to establish an information and consultation forum within a period prescribed by law; and the information and consultation forum should be a standing body, and not one brought into existence intermittently for specific purposes.

7.21 Questions also arise about the nature of the obligation to inform and consult. Implementing legislation should provide that the information and consultation must take place before the decision is taken, and that where the parties fail to agree, it will be necessary to refer the matter to a third party, as in the Netherlands where failures to agree are referred to the Labour Court to resolve. Where a decision is taken without consultation, it should be void and have no legal effect, and wages should continue to be recoverable from the employer: it is not enough to follow the example of the European Works Councils regulations by providing a modest tax deductible fine on employers who fail to comply. One final matter relates to agreements which may be made under the Directive between 'management and labour' by way of opt out form the legislation. Apart from meeting the minimum standards set out in the Directive, only agreements between employers and independent trade unions should be permissible and be recognised for this purpose.

7.22 The Information and Consultation Directive raises again questions which have not been on the agenda for a generation. These include the question of worker representation at higher levels in the corporate structure. It is one thing to be consulted about management proposals, but something again to be involved at an earlier stage with a view to ensuring that proposed job losses are not made in the first place. Systems of co-determination are based on a recognition that many workplaces are individual units within much larger operations, and higher up the organisational hierarchy important decisions are taken which have direct and indirect implications for work and employment at the unit level. In order that attempts to increase workers' participation and rights at the workplace are not undermined by this locus of power beyond the workplace where decisions are based on issues of profitability, workers and trade unions need access to and representation on company boards where these decisions are made. It is time to rekindle the debate about worker and trade union representation on company boards of directors, if only to ensure that the workers' voice is heard when decisions affecting their livelihoods and the welfare of their families are under consideration.

## Recommendations

xi    *The Information and Consultation Directive should be implemented in a way which provides maximum scope for the information to and consultation of workers and their representatives. The implementing legislation should clearly specify when information and consultation should take place.*

xii   *The obligation to inform and consult should apply to all employers to whom the statutory recognition procedure applies (currently those employing at least 21 workers). Where there is a recognised trade union, the obligation to inform and consult workers' representatives on the matters laid out in the Directive should be with the representatives of the recognised trade union, and not otherwise.*

xiii  *All employers to whom the implementing legislation applies should be required to establish an information and consultation machinery by a prescribed date: employers should not be permitted to wait for a request from workers to 'trigger' their obligation. Any decision by the employer taken in breach of the obligation to inform and consult should be void.*

xiv   *In companies which employ more than 500 workers, provision should be made for worker representation on company boards of directors and participation in corporate decision-making. In companies where there is a recognised trade union, the representatives should be nominated by the trade union.*

# Other support for trade union recognition: statutory duties and contract compliance

## Restoring the ACAS statutory duty

7.23 The statutory recognition procedure is only one way by which steps can be taken to promote collective bargaining. It should in fact be only one aspect of a co-ordinated strategy, designed to secure Britain's obligations under international law. There are two principal sources of these obligations. The first is ILO Convention

98 which provides that

> "Measures appropriate to national conditions shall be taken where necessary, to encourage and promote the full development and utilisation of machinery for voluntary negotiation between employers or employers' organisations and workers' organisations, with a view to the regulation of terms and conditions of employment by means of collective agreements."

Given the fact that less than half of British workers are now covered by a collective agreement and that Britain has the lowest collective bargaining coverage in Europe, it can hardly be claimed that measures to promote collective bargaining in this country are 'unnecessary'. The other obligation arising under international law is to be found in the Council of Europe's Social Charter of 1961. This provides that 'with a view to ensuring the effective exercise of the right to bargain collectively, the Contracting Parties undertake,

> "to promote, where necessary and appropriate, machinery for voluntary negotiations between employers or employers' organisations and workers' organisations, with a view to the regulation of terms and conditions of employment by means of collective agreements."

7.24 Consistently with these obligations, it was previously the case that ACAS was charged with the specific statutory duty to promote collective bargaining. But that obligation was removed in 1993, and has not been restored despite the acknowledged role of ACAS in the statutory recognition procedure. The role of the State as described in the White Paper *Fairness at Work* is no longer to promote and encourage collective bargaining, but rather to 'enable trade unions to be recognised for collective bargaining where the relevant workforce chooses such representation', while always recognising that 'many employers and employees will continue to choose direct relationships without the involvement of third parties' (para 1.9). These third parties are presumably trade unions, and the government evidently does not see it as part of its responsibilities to comply with its international obligations in these cases. Given this background, it is hardly surprising that the CAC should be under no duty to promote collective bargaining, despite its role as arbiter of the statutory recognition procedure. Apart from the specific duties to decide on admissibility, bargaining units, majority membership and the like, the only general duty of the Committee is to 'have regard to the object of encouraging and promoting fair and efficient practices and arrangements in the workplace', which is nothing like the duty which ACAS previously operated under.

# Contract compliance

7.25 One way by which trade union recognition can be encouraged is through the power of contract and licence. Those who award contracts or licences could make it a condition of the contract or licence that the contractor or holder of the licence recognises a trade union. This includes public authorities (such as central and devolved government, local authorities and London, national health service bodies, education authorities and universities). It also includes public utility regulators (such as OFGEM, OFWAT, and soon OFCOM), and companies such as Railtrack which provide or maintain public services often through the use of sub-contractors. But it is not only public bodies or companies delivering public services which enter into contractual relations with others for the delivery of goods and services. In the private sector too contracts of this kind for the supply of many and varied products are of course common place.

7.26 There are several reasons why it could easily be justified for a contractor or licensor to require that a contractor or licence holder must recognise a trade union as a condition of the contract or licence. A requirement of this kind would promote security and stability of employment, safe and healthy working practices, and gender equality in the workplace, three public policy goals which are more likely to be found in unionised than non-unionised workplaces. Yet as matters currently stand it is unlawful for such a term to be included in a commercial contract, a statutory provision which is a major violation of the freedom of contract. This provision (now contained in the Trade Union and Labour Relations (Consolidation) Act 1992, s 186) should be repealed so that parties are free to include terms which require work to be done only by contractors or licence holders who recognise an independent trade union. Indeed it ought to be a requirement of public bodies issuing contracts or licences, as well as private companies operating public services, that preference will be given in the award of contracts to companies which recognise an independent trade union.

## Recommendations

xv The duty of ACAS to encourage the extension of collective bargaining and the development of collective bargaining machinery should be restored; and it should be clearly specified in the statutory recognition procedure that the purpose of the procedure is to promote the extension of collective bargaining.

xvi Public authorities and public utility regulators should be required when awarding contracts and issuing licences to take into *consideration whether the businesses to be awarded the contract or licence recognise trade unions.*

*xvii  In the private sector it should be permissible to contract with another party only on the condition that the party in question recognises a trade union. It should be permissible for a trade union to take industrial action to put pressure on an employer to contract only with companies which recognise trade unions.*

## Other support for collective bargaining: multi-employer bargaining and the extension of collective agreements

7.27  The concern so far has been with the rights of trade unions to represent members in particular workplaces, and to secure recognition from individual employers. But one explanation for the low level of collective bargaining coverage in this country when compared with the rest of Europe is that bargaining is conducted on a plant by plant rather than an industry by industry basis. The higher the level at which bargaining is conducted, the higher the likely levels of coverage. The only major countries with collective bargaining density lower than the United Kingdom are Canada, Japan, and the United States where collective bargaining is also conducted – if at all – predominantly at enterprise level. This is a problem which has grown in recent years, as a result of privatisation and the decentralisation of pay determination in the public sector.

7.28  There are many benefits claimed for enterprise based and decentralised bargaining: it enhances flexibility, and provides employers more control over working conditions. But it weakens trade unions by requiring unions to negotiate separate agreements with a large number of sometimes small employers. In the civil service where there was until recently national bargaining, there are now multiple bargaining units which have to be covered by separate agreements. It is true that employers are unlikely to respond to concerns about the problems encountered by trade unions. But there are other reasons why in some industries multi employer or sectoral bargaining would be desirable. Multi - employer bargaining would

- eliminate the destructive wage competition which is currently evident in the railway industry;
- reduce the gender pay gap, with all evidence showing that women do better where pay determination is centralised;
- respond more effectively to health and safety concerns (including working time) by enabling an industry wide strategy to develop;
- encourage the co-ordination of sector-based training, thereby pro-

viding employers and unions with an opportunity to take greater responsibility;

- permit industry wide initiatives to be taken in relation to pensions, which could be provided and managed on a sectoral basis.

7.29 The difficulty arises in how to rebuild the shattered national bargaining structures which at one time operated in this country. For this to work effectively, it has to be through organisations representative of individual trade unions and employers. But it is sometimes said that the employers' associations no longer exist and that trade union structure is no longer conducive to industry wide bargaining. One way forward would be for legislation to require ACAS to encourage the development of multi-employer procedures, and for a similar duty to be imposed on the utility regulators. It would also be possible to amend the statutory recognition procedure so that a union could bring a recognition complaint against more than one employer. This would be very different from the existing procedure which allows a complaint to be brought against only a single employer and only where there is not already a recognised trade union in place. An amendment could allow a trade union which is recognised by two or more employers to bring a recognition application against these employers for a single bargaining unit, which would require the support in a ballot of each of the different workforces. Majority support in the ballots would require the parties to establish a single procedure agreement to cover all the employers balloted.

7.30 In this way it would be possible for a trade union or trade unions to use a statutory procedure to reduce the number of bargaining units. It would still be necessary for bargaining to be conducted at enterprise or company level as well to deal with matters peculiar to particular workplaces and to ensure that any agreements struck with several employers were applied sensibly in specific locations. But even though it would be possible in this way to use the law to rebuild slowly multi-employer procedures, there are other steps that could be taken to ensure that agreements concluded under procedures of this kind had the widest possible application. Thus, where a multi-employer agreement concluded either voluntarily or under the proposed procedure covers a substantial proportion of the workforce, it ought to be possible for the union and the employers who are party to the agreement to apply to the CAC to have it extended to all employers and workers in the industry in question. The agreement would have the effect of setting minimum terms to be applied by all employers in the sector, though they would of course be free to pay more if they chose to do so.

## Recommendation

*xviii Steps should be taken to promote multi-employer bargaining, through a combination of administrative and legal means. Both ACAS and the utility regulators should be under a duty to promote multi-employer bargaining, and the statutory recognition procedure should be amended to allow for the creation of multi-employer bargaining units. A procedure should be introduced for the extension of multi employer collective agreements to all workers in the industry or sector covered by the agreements in question.*

# Conclusion

## The right to be represented by a trade union

i    Workers should have a right to be represented in grievance or disciplinary proceedings by the person of their choice, and to be given a reasonable opportunity during working time to consult the representative and prepare for the hearing.

ii   The right to representation should apply to all matters relating to the employment relationship. It should not be confined to discipline or grievances about existing duties of the employer. A worker seeking to renegotiate the terms of his or her contract should be entitled to be represented when doing so.

## The right of collective representation

iii  Where an independent trade union does not have a majority in membership in a particular workplace to qualify for recognition under the statutory procedure, individual workers should have the right to be collectively represented by their independent trade union.

iv   The right of workers to be represented collectively by an independent trade union should apply only where there is no other independent trade union which is recognised by the employer for the workforce as a whole, either voluntarily or under the statutory procedure. Where there is a recognised union, representational rights should be exercised only by that union.

## The right to trade union recognition

v    The statutory procedure should be revised in order to promote the objective set out in the White Paper *Fairness at Work*. The revisions should specifically: (a) remove the restriction that the procedure applies only to employers of more then 21 workers; (b) remove the ability of employers to defeat applications under the procedure by granting 'recognition' to non independent trade unions; (c) dilute the requirement that bargaining units should be 'compatible with effective management'; (d) remove the power of the

CAC to order a ballot where the union has majority membership; (e) remove the 40 per cent rule in a recognition ballot whereby trade unions must demonstrate not only majority support but also the support of at least 40 per cent of the workers in the bargaining unit; (f) expand the range of collective bargaining issues to which the procedure applies beyond pay, hours and holidays; and (g) reduce to one year the waiting period before another application can be made by the same union in respect of the same bargaining unit.

## Combatting anti-unionism: discrimination and unfair labour practices

vi    The Ullswater amendment allowing employers to discriminate against trade unionists should be repealed, and it should be made clear in legislation that the protection from discrimination on the ground of trade union membership applies also to discrimination based on the use or enjoyment of trade union services, facilities or benefits. In particular it should be unlawful for an employer to subject any worker to a detriment in any respect on the ground that he or she refuses to enter into a contract which includes terms which differ from the terms of a collective agreement applicable to him or her.

vii   It should be an unfair labour practice for an employer to engage in any form of anti-union activity. The following conduct should be regarded as an unfair labour practice:
      – the surveillance of workers related to trade union membership or activities, or trade union recognition;
      – using defamatory material or provocative propaganda;
      – personal attacks or personalised negative campaigning against individuals;
      – the harassment or intimidation of individuals;
      – issuing threats;
      – refusing a union access to the employer's premises to communicate with a member.
      It should also be regarded as an unfair labour practice (in addition to any other remedy the law currently

provides) to discriminate or dismiss workers because of their trade union membership or activities; or to refuse to co-operate with the CAC. Where an employer is found to have committed an unfair labour practice, the CAC should have the power (a) to impose a financial penalty on the employer; (b) to make an award of compensation to any workers affected; (c) to reinstate any worker who has been dismissed; (d) to waive where the circumstances so warrant any of the admissibility requirements for the bringing of an application under the statutory protection (such as the requirement of 10 per cent membership); (e) to permit a trade union to re-submit any unsuccessful application without the need to comply with the existing three year rule; and (f) where appropriate to award recognition without the need for a ballot.

### Rights of recognised trade unions

viii A recognised trade unions should have the right to refer a complaint to the CAC about time off and facilities provided to its workplace representatives by an employer. The CAC should be empowered to determine the content of an agreement.

ix A recognised trade union should have the right to be consulted by the employer on matters relating to training at the workplace. Where there is no recognised trade union, employers should be required to consult with the information and consultation body established under the Information and Consultation Directive.

x A recognised trade union should have the right to be consulted by an employer before any change is made to the pension arrangements of the workers in the bargaining unit. Where there is no recognised trade union, employers should be required to consult with the information and consultation body established under the Information and Consultation Directive. There should be no right on the part of an employer unilaterally to vary pension provisions.

### The right to information, consultation and participation

xi The Information and Consultation Directive should be

implemented in a way which provides maximum scope for the information to and consultation of workers and their representatives. The implementing legislation should clearly specify when information and consultation should take place.

xii The obligation to inform and consult should apply to all employers to whom the statutory recognition procedure applies (currently those employing at least 21 workers). Where there is a recognised trade union, the obligation to inform and consult workers' representatives on the matters laid out in the Directive should be with the representatives of the recognised trade union, and not otherwise.

xiii All employers to whom the implementing legislation applies should be required to establish an information and consultation machinery by a prescribed date: employers should not be permitted to wait for a request from workers to 'trigger' their obligation. Any decision by the employer taken in breach of the obligation to inform and consult should be void.

xiv In companies employing more than 500 workers, there should be worker representation on company boards of directors and participation in corporate decision-making. In companies where there is a recognised trade union, the representatives should be nominated by the trade union.

## Other support for trade union recognition: statutory duties and contract compliance

xv The duty of ACAS to encourage the extension of collective bargaining and the development of collective bargaining machinery should be restored. It should be clearly specified in the statutory recognition procedure that the purpose of the procedure is to promote the extension of collective bargaining.

xvi Public authorities and public utility regulators should be required when awarding contracts and issuing licences to take into consideration whether the businesses to be awarded the contract or licence recognise trade unions.

xvii In the private sector it should be permissible to contract with another party only on the condition that

the party in question recognises a trade union.
It should be permissible for a trade union to take
industrial action to put pressure on an employer to
contract only with companies which recognise trade
unions.

## Other support for collective bargaining: multi-employer bargaining and the extension of collective agreements

xviii  Steps should be taken to promote multi-employer
bargaining, through a combination of administrative
and legal means. Both ACAS and the utility regulators
should be under a duty to promote multi-employer
bargaining, and the statutory recognition procedure
should be amended to allow for the creation of multi-
employer bargaining units. A procedure should be
introduced for the extension of multi employer
collective agreements to all workers in the industry or
sector covered by the agreements in question.

# Chapter 8

# Fairness and security at work

8.1 Britain has some of the weakest employment protection laws of any developed industrial nation when it comes to safeguarding the economic interests of employees in their jobs. We also have a corporate governance system which encourages employers to treat employees as a disposable cost, rather than as an investment for the future. Downsizing, in turn, is a factor in the well-documented increase in ill-health and stress at work in Britain over the past 20 years. As long as this situation persists, insecurity of employment will continue to grow. At the same time, we are unlikely to see sustained improvements in productivity. This situation needs to be addressed by changes to the law and practice governing takeover bids, strengthening employee voice in the takeover process, safeguarding employee rights in relation to transfers and insolvencies, and introducing stronger sanctions against downsizing.

8.2 Employees also have significant sources of 'financial capital' in the form of rights under pension schemes. However, the present legal framework inadequately protects employees' expectations that employers will pay out on the 'pension promise'. It also prevents employees from holding employers and their agents effectively responsible for the management of pension funds, with adverse consequences for the conduct of corporate governance. Changes to law are required in order to firm up the commitments of employers under occupational pension schemes, and to improve mechanisms of accountability in the management of pension assets. We will now consider these issues in more detail, together with proposals for the reform of unfair dismissal law which fails adequately to protect the legitimate expectations of employees from harsh treatment by their employers, and redundancy law which currently fails to provide for effective compensation and consultation rights.

# Re-regulating takeovers

8.3 A large proportion of UK productive capacity, in relative terms, is held in the form of publicly-listed companies: that is to say, companies whose shares are listed on the London stock exchange and/or on one or more of a number of overseas exchanges. The principal shareholders are institutions – insurance companies and pension funds – who invest on behalf of their policy-holders and beneficiaries. They vest the day-to-day control and management of their shareholdings in fund managers who act as their agents. In general, dispersed shareholder ownership encourages shareholders to use exit rather than voice as the mechanism by which shareholders can call management to account. A hostile takeover provides a particularly powerful mechanism for aligning managerial decision-making with shareholders' interests.

## The priority of shareholders

8.4 For a hostile bid to be successful, it is normally necessary for the bidder to offer the shareholders a significant premium over the market price of their shares. In order to recoup its costs, a successful bidder almost invariably engages in major asset disposals and the downsizing of the workforce after the takeover has gone through. The short-term gains to the 'target' shareholders are often offset by losses to employees and other stakeholders. This occurs, in large part, because these other stakeholders are excluded by law from having any meaningful say in the takeover process. The main purpose of the City Code on Takeovers and Mergers is to ensure that all shareholders are treated equally during a bid. At the same time, the Takeover Code and related rules play an important part in entrenching the pursuit of *shareholder value* as the dominant objective of corporate management. To see how this occurs, it is necessary to consider the role of the Takeover Code in supplementing basic company law on directors' duties.

8.5 Company law stipulates that directors must act in good faith in the interests of the *company*, rather than the shareholders, which means that boards have considerable leeway in taking a long-term view of what is in the best interest of stakeholders as a whole. This is reinforced by legislation requiring boards to consider the interests of employees alongside those of shareholders when exercising fiduciary duties (Companies Act 1985, s 309) as well as by case-law recognising that creditors, too, have claims as residual owners when the company approaches insolvency. As a result, boards are permitted to take a view based on 'enlightened shareholder value' – which seeks to strike a balance between the competing interests of the different stakeholders – if their objective is to benefit the shareholders in the long run. For example, in most cases, it would be legally open to the directors to pursue a policy of minimum redundancies (to gain the co-operation of the workforce) or a preferred supplier policy (to enhance the quality of supplier relations), if the ultimate objective of these policies is to advance the long-term interests of shareholders.

## Workers neglected

8.6 However, the picture is quite different once the role of the Takeover Code is factored in. The room for manoeuvre of boards of listed companies is now much more limited. During a hostile take-over bid, the boards of target companies are required to assume a neutral stance and offer disinterested advice to shareholders on the financial merits of the bid. Although the rules of the Code require bidders to state their intentions with regard to the future treatment of employees, this results in little more than the insertion of a stan-dard-form legal 'boilerplate' in offer documents. There is no obliga-tion on the part of either the target board or the board of the bidder company to consult employee representatives during a bid; this only occurs after a bid has gone through when large-scale redundancies are announced. Employee representatives have no standing before the City Panel on Takeovers and Mergers which, despite the power it exercises, is outside the regular court system and almost immune from judicial review. There is also doubt as to how far boards may go in providing information to employee representatives without con-travening the provisions of the Code and the Stock Exchange Listing Rules on the disclosure of price-sensitive information.

8.7 In short, there are strong incentives for boards to prioritise short-term shareholder interests over other interests during a bid. In addition, the prevailing system of executive compensation in the UK provides incentives for boards to engage in hostile take-over activity. By international standards, there is a high level of hostile take-over activity in the UK. Even so, the numbers of hostile bids in a given year will be in the tens rather than the hundreds, whereas the num-ber of listed companies runs into the thousands. More significant is the long shadow cast over corporate governance by the Code and by the listing rules. No listed company is immune from the possibility of a hostile bid. To varying degrees, companies can insulate them-selves against short-term fluctuations in their share price relative to the market by cultivating a culture of long-term investment. But this is not an option open to all; and there is question as to whether it is continuously available for any. In practice, the take-over mechanism has been the principal catalyst for corporate restructuring in the UK during the last decade. Virtually no industrial or services sector has escaped the changes induced by takeover activity.

## The need for change

8.8 The operation of the rules relating to takeover bids has important implications for employment law. As things currently stand, there are a number of weaknesses concerning the practice of the City Panel on Mergers and Takeovers.

- The terms of the City Code relating to employee interests are too loosely drafted. The requirement that bidders should state, in their offer documents, their intentions with regard to the workforce means very little in practice. It should be replaced by a legally binding requirement to the effect that, once a bid has been formally mounted, the boards of the bidder and target companies should come under a duty to inform relevant employee representatives of the potential implications of the bid, and to consult, with a view to reaching an agreement, over the effects of any bid for the workforce. This would involve adapting the existing model of consultation over transfers (subject to this also being strengthened, see below) to takeovers (a takeover by share transfer is, anomalously, not covered by TUPE).

- The City Panel is not adequately accountable through the regular court system for its decisions. Judicial review is not available in any but the most extreme cases. Although the Panel has recently been brought within the general framework of financial regulation (in the sense of being endorsed by the Financial and Services Authority), it is unsatisfactory that a body whose decisions have far-reaching social and employment consequences should not take those factors into account in its decision-making processes. There should therefore be provision for the procedures of the Panel to be amended to make provision for employee representatives to have standing before it.

- The content of the City Code needs to be clarified with respect to the general law governing directors' duties. As we have seen, the City Code places much greater emphasis on shareholders' short-term interests than the general law relating to the fiduciary duty of directors. The Code should be amended in order to make it clear that the directors of a company are able to take a long-term view of the company's interests during the period of a takeover bid, even to the extent of recommending against acceptance of a bid which will benefit the shareholders in the short term.

- Other measures should be considered as part of a general effort to reduce the unhealthy emphasis on the pursuit of short-term shareholder value by corporate boards. The law should take more positive steps to encourage boards to take a view based on what the Company Law Review has called 'enlightened' or long-term shareholder value. A first step would be to strengthen the duty of directors to have regard to the interests of employees when exercising their fiduciary duties (s 309). At present, because employee representatives have no standing to challenge board decisions for breach of this provision, section 309 is invoked only when boards themselves wish to avoid scrutiny by shareholders. Means of providing for employee standing should therefore be considered, alongside the wider reform of intra-corporate litigation which is currently going on as part of the Company Law Review process.

### Recommendations

i  *Following the announcement of a takeover bid for control of a publicly listed company, the boards of the bidder and target should be required to enter into information and consultation processes with employee representatives;*

ii  *Worker representatives should have standing before the City Panel on Mergers and Takeovers;*

iii  *Company law should make it clear that directors can take into account the long-term interests of all the stakeholders when deciding how to respond to a takeover bid; and*

iv  *Worker should have standing before the courts to challenge directors' decisions which ignore stakeholder interests, where these amount to a breach of fiduciary duties under the Companies Act 1985, s 309.*

# Workers' rights in relation to transfers and insolvency

8.9 Under the Transfer of Undertakings (Protection of Employment) Regulations 1981 (TUPE), employers come under obligations to inform employee representatives of (among other things) 'any measures envisaged in relation to the employees' and 'to consult the representatives... in good time on such measures with a view to reaching an agreement'. These information and consultation provisions supplement similar measures under the EC Collective Redundancies Directive (implemented in the Trade Union and Labour Relations (Consolidation) Act 1992, s 188), which arise when an employer proposes to dismiss for redundancy 20 or more employees in a single establishment within a period of 90 days or (in effect) 10 per cent of the relevant workforce over a period of 30 days. These provisions are particularly important where the employer becomes insolvent, or where the possibility of insolvency leads to the sale of the business. TUPE, rather than the Takeover Code, is in point here, since there may be no point in investors acquiring an interest in the share capital of a failing business (although this may depend on the circumstances). It is more likely that the business will be sold as a going concern, which normally triggers TUPE since there will have been a 'relevant transfer' from one employer to another. This means that the new employer inherits the employment law obligations of the transferor.

## The threat to workers' rights

8.10 Following the decision of the House of Lords in *Wilson v St. Helens BC/Baxendale v British Fuels*, where a firm transfers all or part of its business assets, the transferee is not bound to take the employees of the transferor into its employment. The compensation payable by transferees may however be substantial, in particular if it is coupled with liability under the protective award. However, there is growing pressure to exempt insolvency or near-insolvency situations from the coverage of TUPE. Article 5 of the Acquired Rights Directive, which was introduced in 1998, permits a Member State to make provision for a partial derogation from the protective ambit of the Directive. This may only be done during 'insolvency proceedings which have been opened in relation to a transferor (whether or not those proceedings have been instituted with a view to the liquidation of the assets of the transferor) and provided that such proceedings are under the supervision of a competent public authority (which may be an insolvency practitioner determined by national law)'. In addition, a Member State may take advantage of the derogation in the case of 'any transfers where the transferor is in a situation of serious economic crisis, as defined by national law, provided that the situation is declared by a competent national authority and open to judicial supervision, on condition that such provisions already exist in national law by 17 July 1998'.

8.11 In a consultation document issued in 2001, the government proposes a number of changes to TUPE which reflect this new orientation in the ARD. These include: 'clarifying' the law so as to allow for transfer-related changes to terms and conditions of employment provided that they relate to an 'economic, technical or organisational reason'; in insolvency situations, shifting the liability for certain employment-related debts of the transferor from the transferee to the National Insurance Fund; and, again in an insolvency situation, allowing terms and conditions of transferred employees to be modified by agreement between the transferee and appropriate representatives of the employees, where this is done in order to ensure the survival of the undertaking or part of it. The experience of the Rover case in 2000 suggests that bargaining over the application of TUPE can be a means of achieving flexibility within the operation of the law, while still maintaining a role for employment rights in channelling the bargaining process in favour of an inclusive, stakeholder-orientated outcome. In that case, it appears that the Phoenix consortium, which took over the company when the bid by the venture capital firm Alchemy was withdrawn, entered into negotiations with employee representatives, which led to agreement on how to deal with potential claims arising out of breaches by BMW (Rover's former parent) of the law governing consultation and transfers. However, a vital point to bear in mind is that the negotiations which went on in relation to Rover did not require the kind of formal derogation contained in Article 5 of the Directive.

## The need for reform

8.12 There should be scope for bargaining over the application of acquired rights in cases where this would help save jobs which would otherwise be lost. However, it is open to question whether the government's proposals strike the right balance between the need for flexibility in the application of the law, and the need to protect employees' rights against the effects of a restructuring.

- First, the present law is not as strong as it is sometimes said to be. Following the *Wilson/Meade* decision, it seems that transferees are not under an obligation to offer continuing employment to workers dismissed in advance of the transfer they are merely obliged to pay them compensation should they fail to do so. If there is to be collective bargaining over employment rights, it should be against a backdrop of an otherwise enforceable right to continuing employment on the part of the workers affected.

- Secondly, as in other areas of law, there are inadequate safeguards for the protection of employee rights in situations where there is no recognised, independent trade union to bargain on their behalf. It is unlikely that an agreement reached by the transferee with ad hoc representatives of the workers will be one based on effective countervailing power. If collective bargaining is to be allowed to derogate from statutory rights, this should be on the basis of the involvement of an independent trade union.

### Recommendations

*v   Workers affected by a transfer should have the right to be re-employed by the transferee, and not simply a right to be compensated if they are not taken on;*

---

*vi   Any derogations from rights under TUPE in the cases of insolvency and restructuring should be negotiated by an independent trade union; workforce agreements or individual agreements should not suffice to waive statutory rights.*

# Security at work:
# the standard of fairness in dismissal

8.13  As the exemplar of the exercise of managerial prerogative, the power to dismiss commands strong support from the courts. After the Conservative government first introduced protection against unfair dismissal in its Industrial Relations Act, 1971, it took the courts only until the early 1980s, the heyday of Thatcherism, to reassert the dominance of employer authority over and within the modest statutory regime. The 1971 Act allowed a limited set of grounds for which dismissal might be permitted, such as redundancy, misconduct, and poor performance. However the catchall of 'some other substantial reason' was expanded to authorise dismissal in almost any circumstances including events unconnected with work and, crucially, business reorganisation even in the face of the employer's breach or repudiation of the contract of employment. These and other rulings reduced the employer's first hurdle of proving a permitted ground to a minor evidential inconvenience, to the extent that a tribunal could *reject* the employer's pleaded ground yet uphold the dismissal for a different 'real' reason.

## Workers' rights diminished

8.14  The second hurdle, that the employer had acted reasonably in dismissing the employee for a permitted reason, was also undermined. Case law permitted an employer to succeed by establishing a genuine albeit mistaken belief in the employee's 'guilt' provided it was grounded in reasonable evidence following an investigation into the facts. In addition, the judicially devised 'range of reasonable responses' test (RORR) protects employers by imposing a perversity test, in that it describes the area inside which a dismissal is permitted and limits the area outside to what no reasonable employer would have done. It transforms the statutory test into whether it is *possible* that the employer acted reasonably. RORR also sits uneasily with the statutory requirement for equity, or fairness, and allows Tribunals no space within which to have regard to the injustice to the employee (despite the clear wording of the statute). In these ways, the RORR test widens the gap between the public perception of the protection the law affords against dismissal and the reality in tribunals throughout the country.

8.15 One area where the courts were eventually prepared to hold some sort of line concerns the need for employers to follow some degree of fair procedures. Case law does not allow employers to escape by arguing that following proper procedures would have made no difference to the decision to dismiss. This modest protection is now under attack from the Labour government's Employment Act 2002 which will reinstate the any difference test provided the employer has observed minimalist and skeletal procedures. Furthermore, the any difference test survives in the consideration of remedies, so that a finding of unfair dismissal frequently goes hand in hand with an award of little or even no compensation. This combines with the elimination of re-employment, notwithstanding the statutory preference for it as the primary remedy, and with the failure to maintain or restore the real value of the limits on compensation. So unfair dismissal law has followed the same trajectory as much of British business and industry. Instead of competing by enhancing the skills and security of their employees, employers undercut their competitors' treatment of their workforce in a downward spiral of falling standards. In the same way, the law remains wedded to the 1980s' hire and fire economy (*aka* flexibility), protecting employers' unilateral variations to contractual terms and recourse to dismissal as key tools in competition.

## Strengthening workers' rights

8.16 Over 30 years, the judiciary has through interpretation deregulated dismissal law to the point of minor inconvenience for all save the most reckless or ill-informed employer. The failure to reform unfair dismissal law and the retention of a one-year qualifying period will be aggravated by the partial restoration of the any difference test as a sop to the employers' lobby. There is no longer any pretence at striking a balance between the interests of employer and those of the employee. To restore some degree of fairness and security to the law of unfair dismissal, the requirement of 12 months' service before a claim can be made should be removed, and the permitted grounds for dismissal must be more firmly delineated. For example, it should no longer be open to an employer to defend a mistaken belief that the employee was redundant, or had committed some misconduct or failed to perform to the standards required by their contract. Instead, the employer should have to satisfy the tribunal on the balance of probabilities that the employee had committed the offence for which he/she was dismissed or that the other circumstances relied on did actually exist.

8.17 In addition to the foregoing, procedures should be restored to centre stage. The standards in the ACAS Code of Practice should be a minimum requirement, relevant breaches of which should render a dismissal unfair. Most importantly of all, RORR should be replaced with a test of proportionality. Was the dismissal of the employee a proportionate response to the situation? This would not only restore an objective test of fairness, but also introduce the modern European standard of judging whether the employer's action was measured and justifiable. It would become possible to complain of dismissal even where the employee had been at fault. Lastly, the ACAS arbitration system introduced in the Employment Rights (Dispute Resolution) Act 1988 should be open to applicants on a unilateral basis, so that the employer could not force the employee into a tribunal against his/her will. The arbitration route is more likely to produce an industrial solution to dismissal cases, including an effective remedy of re-employment.

### Recommendations

vii    *It should not be necessary as a condition of bringing an unfair dismissal application that the worker had been employed for 12 months.*

viii   *In an unfair dismissal action for misconduct, the employer should have the burden of showing on the balance of probabilities that the employee actually committed the alleged offence;*

ix     *It should be automatically unfair dismissal for an employer to breach the standards laid down in the ACAS Code of Practice relating to discipline and dismissal;*

x      *The 'range of reasonable responses' test in unfair dismissal should be replaced by a test of whether the employer's conduct was objectively justifiable; and*

xi     *It should not be lawful for an employer to require a dismissed worker to take a claim to arbitration rather than have it settled by an employment tribunal.*

# Workers' rights in relation to redundancy

8.18 Current domestic law operates with reference to two different definitions of redundancy. One definition applies to collective redundancy consultation under the provisions of the Trade Union and Labour Relations (Consolidation) Act 1992 and derives from a broad European understanding of redundancy as defined in the Collective Redundancies Directive. This definition focuses on dismissals that arise for a reason not related to the individual concerned. The other definition relates to redundancy payments under the provisions of the Employment Rights Act 1996 and derives from a narrow domestic understanding of redundancy. This definition focuses on the disappearing business, workplace, or job. These two definitions produce an anomaly whereby employees can be considered as redundant for consultation purposes but not in respect of redundancy payments. For example, an employer may have no fluctuation in the demand for work or workers, but wish to dismiss and re-employ categories of staff to harmonise the terms and conditions of employment of the workforce as a whole. The dismissed employees could have a legal right to be consulted, but would have no right to statutory redundancy payments.

8.19 In addition to these definitional differences in the legislation, domestic case law has created a degree of confusion relating to the definition of redundancy for the purpose of redundancy payments contained in the Employment Rights Act 1996, s 139(1)(b), and whether "the requirements of that business for employees to carry out work of a particular kind... have ceased or diminished". After the development of 30 years of case law relating to the correct analysis of this statutory provision, the House of Lords in *Murray v Foyle Meats Ltd* considered that the wording is 'simplicity itself'. It was suggested that the test was to be equated to whether requirements for employees with those particular skills and abilities had ceased or diminished. However, a subsequent judgment of the Court of Appeal in *Shawkat v Nottingham City Hospital NHS Trust (No.2)*, having regard to the decision in Murray, suggested the analysis should be of whether the amount of work and the number of employees to do it had ceased or diminished. This problem of interpretation would be resolved by adopting into redundancy payment legislation the broader Directive definition of redundancy.

## Consultation

8.20 The EC Directive on Collective Redundancies contains two methods for assessing when the duty to consult arises. One method, as adopted by the UK, is where there are 20 redundancies at the same establishment over a 90-day period. The second method is a detailed formula based on 10 per cent of the workforce being made redundant in 30 days. However, Article 5 of the Directive allows Member States to introduce laws, regulations or administrative provisions that are more favourable to workers relating to any provision contained in the Directive. There is thus no need to limit the consultation provisions to cases of 20 redundancies at the same establishment, particularly in light of the problems caused by the meaning of the phrase 'establishment' when assessing the 20-employee threshold. The European Court of Justice in *Rokfon* has ruled that 'establishment' must be understood as meaning the unit to which the workers who have been made redundant have been assigned to carry out their duties. In an industrial relations context this approach would allow an employer who has many units, such as branches or offices, to escape the consultation provisions because 20 or more employees being made redundant within the 90-day period are not assigned to the same unit.

8.21 The Directive provides that, where an employer is contemplating collective redundancies, consultation shall begin in good time with a view to reaching agreement. In *Dansk v H Neilsen & Son,* the ECJ considered that because employees or their representatives are intended to contribute to avoid or reduce redundancies, 'contemplation' should be interpreted in a broad sense and occurs earlier than the 'planning' stage. Domestic legislation, however, requires an employer to consult in good time when redundancies are 'proposed'. Difficulties in reconciling domestic legislation with the Directive were addressed by the EAT in *Scotch Premier Meats v Burns,* where the tribunal considered that it was 'extremely difficult if not impossible' to conclude that 'contemplate' is capable of being construed as meaning 'proposed'. This view has recently been followed by the EAT in *MSF v Refuge Assurance.* The president of the EAT considered that 'contemplation' occurs for the purpose of the Directive when the employer first envisages the possibility, at least as a contingency, that collective redundancies may have to occur. Whereas 'proposes' relates to a state of mind which is much more certain and further along the decision making process than 'contemplation'. Accordingly, the EAT held that it was not possible to construe TULRA in a purposive way that would allow it to accord with the Directive. If this view is correct, then the government has failed properly to implement the Directive into domestic law, which will have to be changed as a result.

## Redundancy pay

8.22 Further areas of concern presented by current redundancy payments legislation surround the calculation of the payment itself. There has been no significant increase in the statutory cap on a week's pay for redundancy payment purposes since it was introduced. Recent changes have ensured that increases in a 'week's pay' are reviewed annually in line with the retail prices index. However, without further change this will only succeed in ensuring that redundancy pay is kept unrealistically low. It is offensive to many that directors in failing businesses receive substantial payments when their services are no longer required, whereas a worker with 30 years' service with a company will currently only receive the statutory maximum redundancy pay of £7,500, which is a sum equivalent to the annual salary of an employee working a 35 hour week on the statutory minimum wage. However, similar arguments of disproportionality were accepted when the amount of the compensatory award was raised to £50,000 in unfair dismissal cases.

8.23 Currently any statutory redundancy payment is calculated with reference to an employee's salary at the time that the redundancy takes effect. This formula is detrimental to those predominantly female employees who change from a substantial period of full-time work to part-time work. In these circumstances the redundancy payment does not reflect the employee's overall contribution to the business and raises concerns of sex discrimination. These points have been rejected by the courts as introducing a restrictively complicated method for employers of calculating redundancy payments and misunderstanding the principle purpose for making a redundancy payment, which the courts concluded should be regarded as compensation for loss of future employment not compensation for past employment. If a redundancy payment is compensation to an employee for the loss of their stake in that particular employment, it is strongly arguable that the 'stake' comprises the skill and expertise acquired by the employee over the whole period of their employment with that employer. For example, a part-time employee may have demonstrated to the employer, over a substantial period of full-time work, significant levels of skill relating to that employer's business. In those circumstances any change in employment from one employer to another cannot be regarded simply in terms of part-time job to part-time job. The 'stake' is loss of future employment with that employer, which has been shaped by the period of past employment.

## Recommendations

*xii*    *Redundancy payment legislation should adopt the broader definition of redundancy contained in the Collective Redundancies Directive. This would remove the current anomaly created by two definitions of redundancy in domestic legislation and also remove the ever-present confusion created by the Employment Rights Act 1996, s 139.*

*xiii*    *An opportunity should be provided for consultation that will allow employees and trade unions to have meaningful input into a consistent and openly fair redundancy process. This would include reducing the 20-employee threshold for collective consultation purposes; re-evaluating the scope of 'establishment' when assessing the collective redundancy threshold; and amending domestic legislation to*

---

*accord with the Directive so consultation begins in good time when dismissals are 'contemplated'.*

*xiv  The amount of a week's pay for redundancy payment purposes should be increased to a level that adequately reflects long service, and a different method of calculating redundancy pay for part-time employees should be created to take into account any significant periods of past full-time work.*

# Protecting workers' pension expectations

8.24  Employees trust their employers to have regard to their interests, and nowhere is the presence of this trust, and the potential for abuse of trust, greater than in the provision, by employers of pensions. Employees expect their pensions to be paid when due, from funds set aside for the purpose. They also regard the pension fund as money held for their benefit, rather than for the employers' benefit. Unfortunately these broad understandings of how a pension scheme will operate bear little relationship to the terms of the legal documentation that employers, through their lawyers, use to set up occupational pension schemes.

## Nature of employers' legal obligations

8.25  While occupational pension schemes represent a long-term trust by employees that their employers will act fairly towards them, the terms of occupational pension schemes have been written so as to represent only a short-term commitment by the employer. Before the government began to restrict the terms of occupational schemes, employers were able to renege on the promise of a pension for any employee who failed to reach retirement whilst still in its employ, there was no minimum level of funding, and companies could walk away from their pension schemes on giving notice (usually as little as six months) leaving the employees with unfunded or only partially funded benefits. As pensions were, and still are, voluntary arrangements that employers are not required to offer, these practices were sought to be justified on the basis that a workforce which had an occupational scheme, however bad, was better off than one that did not. The voluntary nature of occupational pensions also inhibited reforms, as it could be argued that by seeking to improve the terms of occupational schemes, to reduce the gap between members' rights and expectations, employers would be dissuaded from continuing to offer occupational schemes, thereby leaving members worse off.

8.26  The voluntary nature of occupational pension schemes has not prevented government from seeking to reduce this gap. Scheme rules making benefits conditional upon long periods of service with an employer are now prohibited. Insolvent schemes give rise to a debt due from the employer. Rules that give rise to direct and indirect discrimination are overruled. But there is still a long way to go. The Goode Committee tried in 1993 to articulate an understanding of the promise represented by occupational pensions, which it felt was a fair compromise between the terms of existing schemes, and the general understandings and expectations of scheme members. It did not feel able to insist that pension funds were utilised solely for the benefit of scheme members, in the face of the contribution clauses adopted by almost all defined benefit (pensions fixed as a percentage of salary) schemes, which required employers to meet the 'balance of cost'. Where scheme investments perform well, the balance of cost is inevitably reduced, which in turn lowers the employers' contribution rate. Thus where scheme valuations showed surpluses, these were used by employers to lower their contributions, with many employers paying nothing towards their schemes for many years (contribution holidays).

## Holding employers to account

8.27 Rather than attempting to identify a mechanism whereby members could enjoy a fair share of exceptionally good investment returns of the late 80s and 90s, the Goode Committee tried to make employers live up to the promise implicit in their contribution clauses ie. that they would in fact meet the full cost of the promised benefits. Neither the Goode Committee's recommendations, nor the watered-down regulations which followed, ensure that employers actually meet the full cost of the promised benefits. The only mechanism whereby employers could guarantee to pay the defined benefits promised by their schemes is through the purchase of annuities, and these are considered too expensive. So members are not guaranteed their benefits. The solvency standard recommended by Goode (which has yet to be fully introduced and is likely to be abandoned before this occurs) will not ensure that members other than pensioners receive their promised benefits. It only ensures that they receive an amount of assets that, if invested in a money purchase scheme up to their retirement, is likely to earn enough to fund the promised benefits. Instead of guaranteed defined benefits, members have been given a money purchase alternative.

8.28 Future attempts to narrow the gap between expectations and rights are likely to be hampered by employers changing the terms of their schemes, most importantly, by ceasing to offer occupational pension schemes, or by changing from defined benefit schemes which promise a retirement income calculated by an employee's salary, to defined contribution or money purchase schemes where the eventual pension is fixed by reference to whatever sum is produced from accumulated contributions plus investment returns. The justification given by many employers for making these changes is a claim that defined benefit schemes are no longer 'affordable'. The nature of this change, and the reason given for it, point again to the difficulties facing employees in having secure expectations of fair treatment within such a long-term arrangement as a pension scheme. Following years of low or no employer contributions to defined benefit schemes, employers are reluctant to commence making contributions at the levels now required. If employers had a long-term commitment to their occupational schemes, they would not have used high investment returns to fund contribution holidays, but would instead have retained these as reserves to assist funding in periods of lower returns. Unfortunately, a short-term perspective developed in a period of high investment returns, encouraged by tax changes which sought to deter surpluses and accountancy changes which make it more difficult for employers to fund pensions with a constant contribution rate, has conspired to create a situation in which the immediate costs of existing defined benefit schemes are viewed as unaffordable.

## The need for reform

8.29 The cost of funding existing defined benefit schemes could be lowered by altering the formula for awarding benefits, for example, with schemes paying one-sixtieth of salary for each year of service henceforth offering only one-eightieths. This would indicate, in a fairly clear way, the reduction in employers' commitment, and the implications of this for employees. Instead, many employers have preferred to change to money purchase arrangements, with employers contributing less than they calculate would be needed to fund a level of benefit equal to that promised by the replaced defined benefit scheme. By moving from defined benefit to defined contribution schemes employers transfer the risk of low investment return from themselves to their employees, as they no longer have to meet the 'balance of cost'. This move to defined contribution schemes allows employers to reduce the cost of providing pensions in a manner that is less obviously a cut in commitment and cost than a straightforward reduction to the level of benefits within existing defined benefit schemes. In terms of the analysis at the start of this section, the move to defined contribution schemes represents a new opportunity for employers to exploit the gap between employees' general expectation that employers who offer pension schemes are offering security and will treat them fairly and the actual terms of their pension schemes.

8.30 Although employers are already subject to a duty to not to act in a manner likely to destroy their employees' trust in them, and this duty applies to the employer's power under the pension scheme as well as the general contract of employment, this duty offers little protection to employees' expectations. The courts have distinguished between expectations and rights, and treated this duty as something which may operate to prevent rights from being rendered illusory, but does not assist employees who seek to assert claims that cannot be formulated in terms of rights located within statute or trust documents. In this area, as in other parts of the employment relationship, the courts do not generally regard it as a breach of good faith for employers to exercise their powers in order to secure short-term financial gains. A similar attitude has been taken in regard to the power of the Pension Ombudsman to remedy injustice arising from maladministration. This statutory power, which might have been used to ensure that general standards of fairness operated within pension schemes, has been interpreted by the courts so as not to impose standards on employers that are different to those existing under the rules of their occupational schemes, supplemented by statute and European law (subject only to *de minimis* exceptions). The first step in any attempt to ensure fair treatment for employees in the context of pensions is to make occupational pension scheme provision compulsory. Otherwise, the debate on what is fair is always subordinated to employers' perceptions of what they regard as acceptable. Against a background of the compulsory provision and funding of pension schemes, there can be proper debate between trade unions, employers and government on the levels of replacement income, design of benefits, and degrees of security appropriate to pension schemes. Such a debate offers the prospect of employees enjoying expectations that do not diverge as significantly from their legal rights, as they do at present.

### Recommendation

*xv   The law on occupational pension schemes should be changed to make it compulsory for employers to make pension provisions which satisfy minimum standards of security and solvency.*

# Protecting economic security: pension rights

8.31 Employees, through their occupational pension schemes, have billions of pounds invested in companies in the UK and overseas. This represents an enormous amount of shareholder power. In theory the votes which accompany ownership of shares could allow employees through their pension funds to select the membership of boards of directors and to direct the policies of those companies. In practice the workers themselves have very little say in the manner in which their pension funds are invested, and the voting power held by pension funds is rarely exercised. So, for example, if UK pension funds invest in overseas companies with poor labour standards, or ruinous environmental practices, there is very little that the employees can do about it. Until recently, there has been no requirement for employees to participate in decisions on the investment of their deferred pay. As well as a need for workers to participate in decisions made on investment of pension funds, especially those which have direct and indirect effects on their ability to raise labour standards, occupational pensions also raise, in a particularly acute form, the problems of protecting workers who enter into long-term contractual relationships with their employers.

8.32 When employees rely on their employer for their pension arrangements, their rights should not be limited to the strict terms of legal documentation. They need their employer to act in good faith. Indeed, the benefits of pension provision, for both employees and employers, depend to a large extent on the ability of employees to trust their employers to treat them fairly, and for employers not to sacrifice the employees' interests in security to the short-term pursuit of profit. Unfortunately, given the gap between employees' general expectations and the terms of occupational pension schemes, there is a constant danger that such sacrifices will occur. Pension funds operate as trusts, with responsibility for investment entrusted to the trustees. Employees are prevented from influencing the investment strategy of their pension funds by their lack of control over their trustees, and by legal restrictions placed on the behaviour of those trustees. Following the scandal when Robert Maxwell stole £120 million from his employees' pension funds, the Goode Committee recommended that members should be able to appoint at least a third of the trustees of defined benefit (usually final salary) schemes and two-thirds of the trustees of defined contribution or money purchase schemes.

8.33 The first of these recommendations has yet to be implemented in full. Employers are still able to operate alternative arrangements under a statutory regime which places the onus on members to object to these alternatives. The second recommendation, which recognises that with this kind of scheme the whole risk of investment under-performance falls on members rather than the employer, was not accepted. Even in defined contribution schemes, members can only appoint one-third of their trustees, and again only as a default arrangement which operates where they have rejected any alternative offered by their employers. (A particularly worrying situation as increasing numbers of employees are being offered defined contribution schemes.) The employees' current right to appoint a minority of their trustees mean that investment lies in the hands of the majority who are appointed by the employers. These trustees are under no obligation to seek out or respond to the views of their employees as to what constitutes an appropriate basis for making investments. Indeed, as things currently stand, they may be in breach of trust if they do so.

## Recommendation

xvi   *Workers should appoint a majority of the trustees in defined contribution pension schemes, and should have parity with employer representatives in defined benefit schemes. The law should permit pension fund trustees to take due account of social and ethical criteria when taking investment decisions.*

# Conclusion

## Re-regulating takeovers

i   Following the announcement of a takeover bid for control of a publicly listed company, the boards of the bidder and target should be required to enter into information and consultation processes with employee representatives

ii  Worker representatives should have standing before the City Panel on Mergers and Takeovers

iii Company law should make it clear that directors can take into account long-term interests of all the stakeholders when deciding how to respond to a takeover bid

iv  Workers should have standing before the courts to challenge directors' decisions which ignore stakeholder interests, where these amount to a breach of fiduciary duties under the Companies Act 1985, s 309

## Workers' rights in relation to transfers and insolvency

v   Workers affected by a transfer should have the right to be re-employed by the transferee, and not simply a right to be compensated if they are not taken on

vi  Any derogations from rights under TUPE in the cases of insolvency and restructuring should be negotiated by an independent trade union; workforce agreements or individual agreements should not suffice to waive statutory rights

## Security at work: the standard of fairness in dismissal

vii  It should not be necessary as a condition of bringing an unfair dismissal application that the worker had been employed for 12 months.

viii In an unfair dismissal action for misconduct, the employer should have the burden of showing on the balance of probabilities that the employee actually committed the alleged offence

ix   It should be automatically unfair dismissal for an employer to breach the standards laid down in the ACAS Code of Practice relating to discipline and dismissal

x   The 'range of reasonable responses' test in unfair dismissal should be replaced by a test of whether the employer's conduct was objectively justifiable

xi  It should not be lawful for an employer to require a dismissed worker to take a claim to arbitration rather than have it settled by an employment tribunal

## Workers' rights in relation to redundancy

xii  Redundancy payment legislation should adopt the broader definition of redundancy contained in the Collective Redundancies Directive. This would remove the current anomaly created by two definitions of redundancy in domestic legislation and also remove the ever-present confusion created by the Employment Rights Act 1996, s 139.

xiii An opportunity should be provided for consultation that will allow employees and trade unions to have meaningful input into a consistent and openly fair redundancy process. This would include reducing the 20-employee threshold for collective consultation purposes; re-evaluating the scope of 'establishment' when assessing the collective redundancy threshold; and amending domestic legislation to accord with the Directive so consultation begins in good time when dismissals are 'contemplated'.

xiv The amount of a week's pay for redundancy payment purposes should be increased to a level that adequately reflects long service, and a different method of calculating redundancy pay for part-time employees should be created to take into account any significant periods of past full-time work.

## Protecting economic security: pension rights

xv  The law on occupational pension schemes should be changed to make it compulsory for employers to make pension provisions which satisfy minimum standards of security and solvency

xvi Workers should appoint a majority of the trustees in defined contribution pension schemes, and should have parity with employer representatives in defined benefit schemes. The law should permit pension fund trustees to take due account of social and ethical criteria when taking investment decisions

A Charter of Workers' Rights

# Chapter 9

# Enforcement and remedies

9.1 This chapter addresses the need for an overarching and inter-linked strategy for promoting and enforcing employment rights. Such a strategy should deal with ways in which the tribunal system can be made more robust. It also needs to consider, however, other potential means for the enforcement of employment rights. So, for example, we briefly consider issues such as the development of a labour inspectorate, collective enforcement of rights, and various soft law methods of enforcing labour standards such as public procurement, fair wages resolutions, and codes of conduct. Some of these matters have been addressed in earlier chapters but are considered here in more detail as part of a comprehensive package.

9.2 While the content of employment rights are of great importance, paper rights are of no use to anyone if employers do not routinely comply with them. Although there are many workplaces where there is regular compliance with the standards set down in statute or other legal provisions, particularly where trade unions are recognised and active, there are many workplaces where individual and collective rights are breached either on a routine or ad hoc basis. It is therefore necessary for any charter of rights also to put forward some ideas with regard to both the way in which rights are enforced as a last resort through the state machinery of the tribunals and courts, but also look to various ways in which employers are encouraged to comply with employment rights either by resolving any problems about infringement of rights internally or by other means of 'encouragement' such as contract compliance, labour inspectorate and adherence to codes of conduct.

9.3 What is set out below in relation to enforcement mechanisms is not intended to be a menu from which certain possibilities can be selected and others rejected. Nor are some of the proposals intended to be alternative courses of action to more traditional means of enforcement such as trade union action or applications to tribunals. Rather, what is proposed is intended to be a range of overarching and complementary strategic interventions, which between them have a defined aim: first, to secure employment rights for workers and, secondly, only where such rights are not complied with, to ensure that workers have appropriate redress.

# Employment tribunals

9.4 In recent years there has been a substantial debate over the role of tribunals and discussions as to how the number of claims before tribunals can be reduced. The reality is, however, that many of the purported savings and changes that the government is seeking to achieve in relation to tribunals will not in either the short term or long term reduce the number of claims before tribunals. The apparent absence of any alternative means of enforcing employment rights has the effect that workers will still feel that they are the only option to seek industrial justice. This should not surprise anyone. While there may be some arguments that the tribunals could be more focused on occasion, the reality is that compared with many courts they are often too easily criticised. Further, they bring with them the enviable quality of being properly tripartite, and also provide a system that generally is trusted by both employers and worker representatives alike.

### Recommendations

i   *Tribunals should be kept tripartite wherever possible. Efficiency gains achieved by having cases heard by tribunal chairs sitting alone do not compensate for the loss of industrial good sense and knowledge which lay members bring.*

ii  *Any changes to tribunal practice and procedure should only be introduced where it can be shown that they are in the best interests of securing effective justice for workers whose rights have been breached. There may be many alternative means of adjudicating claims more quickly, but the right to seek justice from an independent tribunal as a last resort should not be compromised.*

# Class actions and tribunal orders

9.5 One major gap in the enforcement of employment rights through the tribunal system relates to the ability of tribunals to adjudicate upon issues that affect a wide group of workers quickly, and in a way that ensures all of the workers benefit from any ruling on the issue. This is particularly obvious in respect of equal pay claims, where it is necessary for each individual to lodge a claim and, at least in theory, for each of these claims to be made out. This, combined with the complexity of the law, leads to cases taking an inordinate length of time. Equal pay is not the only area where the subject of the dispute may affect a range of workers. Redundancy is another example. Moreover, while tribunals may make recommendations arising out of the case of the individual claiming before them, there are limitations on their powers to make formal recommendations in respect of the future conduct and action of employers in general – even though the need for an employer to reform their ways and develop decent employment practices may be absolutely clear from the evidence before the tribunal.

### Recommendation

iii *Tribunals should have the right to hear class actions in appropriate cases, with the decision being binding in respect of a defined category of workers. Tribunals should also be given the power in appropriate cases to make recommendations that go beyond the facts of individual cases before them. So, for example, where a tribunal finds that an employer never had a procedure for dismissals in place, the tribunal should be empowered to make a recommendation to the employer that he or she introduce such a procedure, even though the individual in question – namely the person bringing the tribunal case – is no longer employed by the employer. Any subsequent case that was decided against the employer where it was found that the employer had failed to comply with tribunal recommendations could find the employer facing a financial penalty for the failure.*

# Voiding dismissals and other management decisions

9.6 One mechanism to improve the level of enforcement of labour rights is to provide that management decisions made in breach of legal standards are void and ineffective. So, for example, if a dismissal was made in breach of procedures set down in statute of contract, or when a dismissal takes place for unlawful reasons, for example because it was based on discriminatory grounds, that dismissal could be declared by the court or tribunal to be invalid. The obvious attractions of such an approach is that the worker would be placed back in the job with no break in service and treated exactly as if he or she had still been employed throughout any intervening period between 'dismissal' and adjudication. In order to be effective, however, any such adjudication would have to take place very quickly as the longer the time between the dismissal and the adjudication, the more difficulty there would be in placing the worker back in work.

9.7 This simple proposal is aimed not at replacing compensation as the most regular form of remedy for breaches of individual employment rights, but is rather intended to try to ensure that the proportion of employees who find themselves back in the workplace after an unlawful dismissal is higher than the derisory number as a result of the existing reinstatement and re-engagement provisions. Although not ratified by the UK, ILO Convention 158 on the Termination of Employment provides by article 10 that if a dismissal is found to be unjustified by the relevant adjudicatory body, 'if they are not empowered or do not find it practicable, in accordance with national law and practice, to declare the termination invalid and/or order or propose reinstatement of the worker, they shall be empowered to order payment of adequate compensation or such other relief as may be deemed appropriate'. Thus, the Convention, while envisaging the possibility of reinstatement or the nullifying of dismissals, does not require it, provided that compensation or other remedies are available in the alternative.

### Recommendation

iv   *Certain defined categories of dismissal should be regarded as void. Such a finding would have the effect that the dismissal had never taken place. Dismissals regarded as void should include: trade union dismissals; discriminatory dismissals; victimisation dismissals related to the assertion of a range of rights; and any other dismissal in relation to which there is at present no qualifying period for unfair dismissal. It should also be possible for a court or tribunal to declare void any management decisions which have been taken in breach of a defined collective redundancies procedure, and TUPE related decisions. This would require the employer to go back through the procedure in order to make a decision that was valid.*

# Building a labour inspectorate

9.8 The advantages of having some form of investigation-based compliance mechanisms for labour rights are clear. Enforcement, at the end of the day, is the obligation of the State. The State is obliged to ensure, particularly under international law, that fundamental and basic rights are respected, that individuals have a right to complain, and that laws are enforced on a day-to-day basis. The ability of individuals to raise complaints during the course of their employment depends on workers having the ability or inclination to lodge claims. However, this is often far from easy. Worries related to retaining the employment long-term mean that many workers have to put up with poor treatment from their employer. One only has to look at the number of complaints in jurisdictions related to the payment of wages to note that it is predominantly those people who have left employment who bring claims.

9.9 The idea of labour inspectorate was raised in chapter 4 in our discussion of the statutory minimum wage. But clearly a labour inspectorate – whose work could concentrate on the most vulnerable – would have a much wider range of responsibilities, which would not be confined to the statutory minimum wage. These might include the payment of wages, working time, holidays and holiday pay, and payments relating to the exercise of paid maternity and paternity leave. The role of the inspectorate would be to investigate breaches of employment rights, issue notices to employers to require them to comply with employment rights, and to initiate legal proceedings against employers thought to be in breach. A fully-fledged inspectorate of this kind would bring us more into line with established international labour standards. These include ILO Convention 81 (the Labour Inspection Convention (1947)), and the 1995 Protocol to the Convention. The United Kingdom has only partially ratified the Convention and has failed to ratify the protocol. Both should be fully ratified, and implementing legislation introduced as a priority if rights in principle are to mean rights in practice to the most disadvantaged members of thc labour force.

### Recommendation

v    *The labour inspectorate proposed in chapter 4 should have a wide range of enforcement responsibilities. It should be properly resourced and inspectors given the power to impose financial penalties on employers and also, where appropriate, issue remedial instructions. The inspectorate should also be charged with working with ACAS and other organisations to assist employers to comply with employment rights.*

# Soft law – procurement, fair wages, codes of conduct

9.10 There are a number of new initiatives that have emerged over recent years that aim to apply direct or indirect pressure on employers to comply with minimum standards. Within this category of initiatives we include corporate corporate codes of conduct, negotiated sector codes of conduct, and public initiatives such as fair wages resolutions, contract compliance and public procurement measures. The key point about this range of mechanisms is that they seek either to use contractual relations or public pressure applied through the market in order to encourage companies and others to comply with defined labour standards. So, for example, in the case of broad-based and well-established initiatives, the Ethical Trading Initiative in the United Kingdom includes non-governmental organisations, trade unions, supermarkets and their suppliers. They have come together to seek to define and develop methods whereby labour standards are complied with throughout the global supply chain.

9.11 Similarly, certain public authorities such as the Mayoral Office of the Greater London Authority, have attempted to encourage their suppliers to comply with certain defined labour standards. The ultimate sanction in all of these cases is cutting off a contract to supply. However, there is also the possibility that employers who trade with companies where standards are substantially in breach of accepted norms will find that the adverse publicity in doing so is bad for business. One of the major advantages of this form of enforcement is that it seeks to do something about the sub-contracting and fragmentation of the labour market, and the difficulty in establishing responsibility for breaches of labour rights that arises in such circumstances. The responsibility for implementing corporate codes of conduct or government procurement policy ultimately lies with the party sitting at the top of the supply chain, which is almost inevitably the most powerful economic actor, whether it be a multinational corporation or a large government department.

## Government action – procurement and fair wages

9.12 There is already some renewed interest in looking to the way that government and other public authorities use their buying and contracting power to influence the labour market. The Greater London Authority is trying to implement fair wages clauses in its contracts with suppliers and others, and the New York City Comptroller's office has a specific Bureau of Labor Law to enforce laws that require private sector contractors engaged in public work projects in the City of New York to pay no less than the prevailing wage to their employees for work covered by the statutes, as determined by that Bureau. There are strong arguments that if it is government policy to encourage business to promote labour rights compliance through corporate social responsibility and codes of conduct, then government itself should use its substantial buying and contracting power to seek to influence compliance with defined labour standards by all those with whom it dies business.

9.13 There are some legal questions that need to be resolved with regard to the scope under European public procurement rules and also national legislation, particularly in relation to the constraints on local government in respect of contracting in the framework of 'Best Value'. However, without going into these rather complex issues, there are legal opinions to the effect that the rules are sufficiently wide to enable public authorities to take labour related matters into account when awarding contracts, subject to the need for some clarification of the UK law in this regard. It should be clearly provided that all contractors should be free to take labour standards into account and obligatory for public authorities to do so. To this end ILO Convention 94 (Labour Clauses in Public Contracts Convention (1949)) should be ratified by the UK. This provides that certain public authorities should contract only with employers observing fair labour standards. Britain's ratification of this Convention was denounced by the Thatcher government in the 1980s.

### Recommendation

vi  *UK legislation should be amended so that it requires public bodies to take the labour standards of contractors and suppliers into account when awarding contracts. The British government should ratify ILO Convention 94.*

# Codes of conduct

9.14 Codes of conduct relating to labour standards in the supply chain have developed substantially over recent years. Many of the first examples of such codes were, essentially, public relations exercises carried out by multinational organisations to try to avoid the embarrassment of being seen to be sitting at the top of a supply chain pyramid built on exploited labour. But some of the more recent initiatives and examples are much more robust attempts to try to use some market levers and powers, coupled with trade union and consumer action, to apply pressure on contractors and suppliers to afford basis labour rights to what are often some of the most vulnerable categories of workers. Although they are by no means an alternative strategy to trade union action and state enforcement, codes of conduct where properly implemented and routinely monitored and inspected can be shown to have some effect in sectors of the economy where previously compliance with employment rights was at best patchy. The possible scope for action here derives from the fact that contractors and others will often cite as the reason why they cannot 'afford' to comply with labour legislation as the pressures placed upon them, commercially, by the party to whom they contract to supply goods or services. Where it is this very party who is demanding that they apply labour standards, then the argument loses at least some of its force. Moreover, the contractor knows that implementing basic rights is an important part of the contract.

9.15 The experience of the Ethical Trading Initiative, and other comparable programmes in other countries, has indicated that codes of conduct are only likely to be successful where they involve trade unions, public authorities and other relevant non-governmental organisations from the outset. It is important to note that codes of conduct like the ETI code were negotiated with substantial trade union input, rather than determined by individual companies. As a minimum all codes of conduct should be: based on ILO labour standards; negotiated with trade unions representing the workers whom the code would protect; in the case of international codes, they should be negotiated with the relevant global union federations; and, finally, should be monitored and verified on a continuing basis in a transparent manner. The development of codes of conduct may be given further emphasis as a result of the European Commission's new strategy on Corporate Social Responsibility that was published in July 2002. Where codes of conduct are successfully implemented they also have the added advantage of making the implementation of labour rights an international, rather than merely domestic issue, as the company in question is obliged to seek improvements through the whole of its international supply chain or contracting network. There is also a need for international co-ordination in this regard to ensure that, where appropriate, trade rules include measures which support the protection of labour rights in the face of the ability of international capital to move from one jurisdiction to another.

## Recommendation

vii   The government should support the development of appropriate codes of conduct on labour standards applicable to private sector companies as part of its overall strategy to promote corporate social responsibility. The government should seek to ensure that trade union organisations are involved in the design and monitoring of codes of conduct. The government and the European Union should seek to ensure that trade rules and the operation of the international financial institutions promote respect for labour rights and that multinational organisations are held accountable where they are responsible for breached of labour standards in their supply chain.

# Conclusion

## Employment tribunals

i     Tribunals should be kept tripartite wherever possible. Efficiency gains achieved by having cases heard by tribunal chairs sitting alone do not compensate for the loss of industrial good sense and knowledge which lay members bring.

ii     Any changes to tribunal practice and procedure should only be introduced where it can be shown that they are in the best interests of securing effective justice for workers whose rights have been breached. There may be many alternative means of adjudicating claims more quickly, but the right to seek justice from an independent tribunal as a last resort should not be compromised.

## Class actions and tribunal orders

iii     Tribunals should have the right to hear class actions in appropriate cases, with the decision being binding in respect of a defined category of workers. Tribunals should also be given the power in appropriate cases to make recommendations that go beyond the facts of individual cases before them. So, for example, where a tribunal finds that an employer never had a procedure for dismissals in place, the tribunal should be empowered to make a recommendation to the employer that he or she introduce such a procedure, even though the individual in question – namely the person bringing the tribunal case – is no longer employed by the employer. Any subsequent case that was decided against the employer where it was found that the employer had failed to comply with tribunal recommendations could find the employer facing a financial penalty for the failure.

## Voiding dismissals and other management decisions

iv     Certain defined categories of dismissal should be regarded as void. Such a finding would have the effect that the dismissal had never taken place. Dismissals regarded as void should include: trade union dismissals; discriminatory dismissals; victimisation dismissals related to the assertion of a range of rights; and any other dismissal in relation to which there is at present no qualifying period for unfair dismissal. It should also be possible for a court or tribunal to declare void any management decisions which have been taken in breach of a defined collective redundancies procedure, and TUPE related decisions. This would require the employer to go back through the procedure in order to make a decision that was valid.

### Building a labour inspectorate

v    The labour inspectorate proposed in chapter 4 should have a wide range of enforcement responsibilities. It should be properly resourced and inspectors given the power to impose financial penalties on employers and also, where appropriate, issue remedial instructions. The inspectorate should also be charged with working with ACAS and other organisations to assist employers to comply with employment rights.

### Government action – procurement and fair wages

vi    UK legislation should be amended so that it requires public bodies to take the labour standards of contractors and suppliers into account when awarding contracts. The British government should ratify ILO Convention 94

### Codes of conduct

vii    The government should support the development of appropriate codes of conduct on labour standards applicable to private sector companies as part of its overall strategy to promote corporate social responsibility. The government should seek to ensure that trade union organisations are involved in the design and monitoring of codes of conduct. The government and the European Union should seek to ensure that trade rules and the operation of the international financial institutions promote respect for labour rights and that multinational organisations are held accountable where they are responsible for breached of labour standards in their supply chain.

# Chapter 10

# Conclusion: a workers' charter

10.1 The preceding analysis and recommendations no doubt omit some points where further significant steps to justice could be made. Nevertheless it can be said with some confidence that fulfilment of these recommendations would bring to an end the unenviable record of the UK as an breaker of the international labour laws which it has ratified. But the list of recommendations is still far too unwieldy for presentation as a workers' charter. It is necessary to have in mind the core principles and values found in chapter 1 and to distil the recommendations into, say, 10 key points which are broad enough to encompass the recommendations and yet not so all embracing as to lose meaning. It is thought that the following rights encapsulate the proposals made and for which this book argues:

### Dignity and fair terms:
The right to dignity at work, to a fair wage and to just conditions of work.

### Health and safety:
The right to a safe and healthy working environment.

### Non-discrimination:
The right not to be discriminated against and to be treated with equality in equivalent circumstances.

### Job security:
The right to security of employment (whether in relation to closures, redundancies, transfers or otherwise).

### Income security:
The right to fair income security in retirement, sickness and unemployment.

## Union membership:

The right to form and join a trade union for the protection of the worker's occupational, social and economic interests, and not to be discriminated against on grounds of union membership, participating in union activities, or union representation.

## Union autonomy:

The right of a union to uphold its own rule-book, to spend its funds and to conduct its activities including industrial action in accordance with its rules, free from employer and state interference.

## Industrial action:

The right to take industrial action for the protection of the worker's occupational, social and economic interests (or those of any other worker) without being in breach of contract, and without threat of dismissal or discrimination.

## Union representation:

The right of individual and collective representation by a trade union, including the right to collective bargaining and to participate in decisions at work.

## Effective remedies:

The right, from the outset of the employment, to effective remedies to enforce these rights, including adequate rights for workers' representatives to inspect and to obtain information.

10.2 These rights need to be incorporated into an Act of Parliament. The government should be required by such legislation to carry out an audit of all the UK's laws to ensure that none conflicts to any extent with international standards embracing these rights. Parliament through the Joint Committee on Human Rights should scrutinise all legislation to ensure conformity with international standards embracing these rights. International standards embracing these rights should be legally enforceable, and the courts must ensure that such rights are not compromised or encroached upon by the rights of others.

# IER's latest publications

The Institute operates a dual pricing policy: the lower price is the cost to subscribers, members, trade unions and students, the second is the cost to other purchasers.

**LABOUR LAW REVIEW 2002** by Jennifer Eady and Rebecca Tuck (£3/£10)

**PROTECTING WORKER SOLIDARITY ACTION: A CRITIQUE OF INTERNATIONAL LABOUR LAW** by Paul Germanotta (£6.50/£20)

**THE EU CHARTER OF FUNDAMENTAL RIGHTS: WASTE OF TIME OR WASTED OPPORTUNITY?** by Keith Ewing (£6.50/£20)

**BETWEEN A ROCK AND A HARD PLACE: THE PROBLEMS FACING FREELANCE CREATORS IN THE UK MEDIA MARKET-PLACE** by Lionel Bently (£8/£30)

**WHISTLEBLOWING AND THE PUBLIC INTEREST DISCLOSURE ACT 1998** by Catherine Hobby (£8/£30)

**UNDERMINING CONSTRUCTION: THE CORROSIVE EFFECTS OF FALSE SELF-EMPLOYMENT** by Mark Harvey (£8/£30)

**COMPARATIVE NOTES 6**
**LABOUR'S LABOUR LAW: LABOUR LAW REFORM IN NEW ZEALAND UNDER A LABOUR GOVERNMENT** by Gordon Anderson (£5/£10)

**LABOUR LAW REVIEW 2001** by Jennifer Eady and Rebecca Tuck (£3/£10)

**BUILDING ON THE NATIONAL MINIMUM WAGE** by Bob Simpson (£6.50/£20)

**EMPLOYMENT RIGHTS AT WORK: REVIEWING THE EMPLOYMENT RELATIONS ACT 1999** edited by Keith Ewing (£12/£30)

**INTERNATIONAL TRADE UNION RIGHTS FOR THE NEW MILLENNIUM** by Keith Ewing and Tom Sibley (£8/£30)

**CHALLENGING RACE DISCRIMINATION AT WORK** by Karon Monaghan (£8/£30)

**FAIRNESS AT WORK? THE DISCIPLINARY AND GRIEVANCE PROVISIONS OF THE 1999 EMPLOYMENT RELATIONS ACT** by Mike Clancy and Roger Seifert (£6.50/£20)

**HUMAN RIGHTS AT WORK** edited by Keith Ewing (£12/£30)

**SOCIAL JUSTICE AND ECONOMIC EFFICIENCY** published in association with the *Cambridge Journal of Economics* (£8/£30)

**CHALLENGING DISABILITY DISCRIMINATION AT WORK** by Mary Stacey and Andrew Short (£6.50/£20)

**COMPARATIVE NOTES 5
RESISTING UNION-BUSTING TECHNIQUES: LESSONS FROM QUEBEC** by Laura Dubinsky (£5/£10)

**EMPLOYMENT RIGHTS: BUILDING ON FAIRNESS AT WORK** (£5/£10)

**COMPARATIVE NOTES 4
TRADE UNION RIGHTS IN SOUTH AFRICA: THE LABOUR RELATIONS ACT 1995** by Roger Welch (£5/£10)

**REGULATING HEALTH AND SAFETY AT WORK: THE WAY FORWARD** edited by Phil James and Dave Walters (£12/£24)

**AGE DISCRIMINATION IN EMPLOYMENT** by Malcolm Sargeant (£6.50/£20)

**COMPARATIVE NOTES 3
DEVELOPING RECOGNITION AND REPRESENTATION IN THE UK: HOW USEFUL IS THE US MODEL?** by Brian Towers (£5/£10)

**LABOUR LAW REVIEW 1999** by Jennifer Eady and Jeremy McMullen QC (£3/£10)

**COMPARATIVE NOTES 2
RESOLVING EMPLOYMENT RIGHTS DISPUTES THROUGH MEDIATION: THE NEW ZEALAND EXPERIENCE AND ACAS ARBITRATION** by Susan Corby (£5/£10)

**FAIRNESS AT WORK AND TRADE UNION RECOGNITION: PAST COMPARISONS AND FUTURE PROBLEMS** by Lord McCarthy (£6.50/£20)

**SURVEILLANCE AND PRIVACY AT WORK** by Michael Ford (£6.50/£20)

**A SOCIAL CLAUSE FOR LABOUR'S CAUSE: GLOBAL TRADE AND LABOUR STANDARDS – A CHALLENGE FOR THE NEW MILLENNIUM** by David Chinn (£6.50/£20)

**INTERNATIONAL LABOUR RIGHTS – NEW METHODS OF ENFORCEMENT** by Steve Gibbons (£6.50/£20)

**ROBEN'S REVISITED – THE CASE FOR A REVIEW OF OCCUPATIONAL HEALTH AND SAFETY REGULATION** by David Walters and Phil James (£6.50/£20)

**LOW PAY AND THE MINIMUM WAGE** by Sanjiv Sachdev and Frank Wilkinson (£6.50/£20)

**IN DEFENCE OF TRADE UNIONISM** by Jim Mortimer (£5/£10)

**COMPARATIVE NOTES 1
TRADITION AND CHANGE IN AUSTRALIAN LABOUR LAW** by Anthony Forsyth (£5/£10)

**EVERY WORKER SHALL HAVE THE RIGHT TO BE REPRESENTED AT WORK BY A TRADE UNION** by John Hendy QC (£8/£30)

**NEED TO BE HEARD AT WORK? RECOGNITION LAWS – LESSONS FROM ABROAD** edited by Keith Ewing (£8/£25)

**WORKER PARTICIPATION AND COLLECTIVE BARGAINING IN BRITAIN: THE INFLUENCE OF EUROPEAN LAW** by Joe O'Hara (£6/£20)

**THE GUIDE TO WORKING LIFE – A NEW PERSPECTIVE ON LABOUR LAW** (£6/£20)

**LABOUR STANDARDS – ESSENTIAL TO ECONOMIC AND SOCIAL PROGRESS** by Simon Deakin and Frank Wilkinson (£6/£20)

**THE LAW ON INDUSTRIAL ACTION UNDER THE CONSERVATIVES** by Dr Sonia McKay (£6/£20)

**INDUSTRIAL ACTION BALLOTS AND THE LAW** by Jane Elgar and Bob Simpson (£6/£20)

**LABOUR LAW AND FREEDOM – FURTHER ESSAYS IN LABOUR LAW** by Professor Bill Wedderburn QC (£19.99)

**TOWARDS THE INSECURITY SOCIETY: THE TAX TRAP OF SELF-EMPLOYMENT** by Dr Mark Harvey (£6/£20)

**WOMEN IN LABOUR: PARENTING RIGHTS AT WORK** by Sandra Fredman (£6/£20)

a complete list of available publications is posted on our website
**www.ier.org.uk**